LAW
BASICS
Student Study Guides

CRIMINAL LAW

FIFTH EDITION

LAW **BASICS**
Student Study Guides

CRIMINAL LAW

FIFTH EDITION

By

Clare Connelly, MA (Hons), LLB, DipLP

Devil, Faculty of Advocates
Senior Lecturer, School of Law, University of Glasgow

W. GREEN   **THOMSON REUTERS**

First Edition published in 2002
Second Edition published in 2004
Third Edition published in 2008
Fourth Edition published in 2010

Published in 2013 by W. Green,
21 Alva Street, Edinburgh EH2 4PS
Part of Thomson Reuters (Professional) UK Limited
(Registered in England & Wales, Company No 1679046. Registered
Office and address for service:
Aldgate House, 33 Aldgate High Street, London EC3N 1DL)

www.wgreen.co.uk

Typeset by Alex Nashed, W. Green, Edinburgh
Printed and bound in the UK by CPI Antony Rowe

No natural forests were destroyed to make this product;
only farmed timber was used and replanted.

A CIP catalogue record of this book is available from the British Library.

ISBN 978-0-414-01926-3

Thomson Reuters and the Thomson Reuters logo are
trademarks of Thomson Reuters.

CONTENTS

TABLE OF CASES

1. INTRODUCTION

Criminal law in the broadest sense incorporates the rules of procedure and substantive criminal law. Rules of procedure govern how cases are progressed through court; substantive criminal law defines crimes and defences. Scottish criminal law is predominantly common law. Common law refers to law that does not stem from a statute and is laid down in authoritative writings and judicial decisions (case law). The substantial body of common law in Scotland is supplemented by some statutes, including the Misuse of Drugs Act 1976, the Road Traffic Act 1984, the Sexual Offences (Scotland) Act 2009 and most recently the Criminal Justice and Licensing (Scotland) Act 2010 (hereafter "CJLSA 2010"). The use of statute to create new crimes or reform the common law is becoming more prevalent. This text is concerned primarily with the common law element of Scottish criminal law but also includes the recent Sexual Offences (Scotland) Act 2009, which has replaced a number of common law sexual offences with statutory offences, and the CJLSA 2010 provisions relating to offences and defences.

THE ADVERSARIAL PROCESS

Scotland has an adversarial process as opposed to an inquisitorial process which is dominant in mainland Europe. In an adversarial process, there are two opposing sides who argue out a dispute before a judge. The judge operates as an umpire or arbiter. The role of the judge is not to question witnesses but to ensure that the rules are followed and should only intervene for this purpose. In *Thomson v Glasgow Corporation* (1961) at p.246 Lord Justice Clerk Thomson summed up the adversarial process as follows:

> "A litigation is in essence a trial of skill between opposing parties, conducted under recognised rules and the prize is the judge's decision. We have rejected inquisitorial methods and prefer to regard our judges as entirely independent. Like referees at a boxing contest, they see the rules are kept and count the points."

WHO DETERMINES WHAT THE CONTEST IS ABOUT?

In an adversarial process, unlike in an inquisitorial process, it is the lawyers rather than the judge who determine which issues are to be litigated. This is primarily done by the prosecutor in a criminal case. It is in response to the case of the prosecutor that the accused does two things:

(1) they may lead evidence that challenges or undermines the case of the prosecutor, e.g. by leading evidence from a witness who

1

provides an alternative account of the incident at issue; or
(2)   they may lead evidence of an issue that is not part of the case constructed by the prosecutor, e.g. a defence of self-defence.

PROSECUTION

There is a system of public prosecution in Scotland. The prosecution is referred to either by that name or the Crown. Private prosecutions are permissible but only under restricted conditions and are very rare. In a public prosecution, the prosecution is brought at the instance of the Lord Advocate in the High Court and of the procurator fiscal in the sheriff or justice of the peace ("JP") courts. The decisions regarding whether a prosecution should be brought, the crime(s) to be charged, the court and form of proceeding are made by procurator fiscal deputes and this process is called "marking". Decisions regarding prosecution cannot be reviewed by the public.

Trials proceed on an indictment in solemn cases and a complaint in summary cases. The charge in an indictment is sometimes called "a libel". Both indictments and complaints contain a statement of the crimes that are to be prosecuted. Cases are differentiated by whether or not a jury is present. Hence, in summary cases, where the charges will involve less serious crimes, a jury is not present and such trials take place in the sheriff or JP courts. In solemn cases, the charges will involve more serious crimes, a jury is present and the trial will take place in either the sheriff court or the High Court.

Fifteen people serve on a jury and the verdict is by majority. Before a person can be convicted of a crime, at least 8 of the 15 jurors must find the accused guilty. Scotland has three verdicts: guilty, not guilty and not proven. Contrary to popular belief, the not proven verdict has the same legal consequences as a not guilty verdict. The principle of res judicata applies equally to a person acquitted on a not guilty verdict as it does to one acquitted on a not proven verdict. Res judicata means "a case or matter decided". The effect of this rule is that, following a verdict in a trial or where the prosecution has deserted a trial, no further prosecutions can be initiated against the accused on the same charges.

Under common law, a jury can convict of an offence which is close to that in the libel and differentiated only in being a lower mode or degree of the same sort of crime, e.g. a conviction of culpable homicide on a charge of murder, or of theft on a charge of housebreaking or of assault on a charge of hamesucken (assault in a person's own home). These common law examples have been supplemented by statute since the late nineteenth century. Such provisions in effect extend the jury's powers to return a modified verdict, by including in the indictment an implied averment of the alternative charge of which the accused may be convicted (*Johnston v HM Advocate* (2009)).

ACCUSED

The age of criminal responsibility in Scotland has been increased from 8 to 12 by the CJLSA 2010 s.38. The administration of criminal justice has a protective function in respect of the accused. The criminal justice system embodies the principles of the presumption of innocence, the right to a fair trial and the availability of legal aid. The principle of res judicata, also known as double jeopardy, namely that a person should not be prosecuted more than once for the same crime, was embodied in statute in 2011 albeit with amendments. The Double Jeopardy (Scotland) Act 2011 creates a number of exceptions to the general prohibition, namely where the original trial was 'tainted' (s.2), where an acquitted accused subsequently admits to the offence (s.3) and where new evidence emerges (s.4). There are also evidential provisions in respect of the onus and burden of proof.

In a criminal trial the onus of proof is on the Crown to prove the guilt of an accused, this is known as the persuasive burden. The only time the law places an obligation or onus upon the accused to produce exculpatory evidence, at common law, is in respect of diminished responsibility and mental disorder (previously known as insanity) and there are also some statutory provisions that impose such an obligation on the accused. So, where the defence of mental disorder or diminished responsibility is pled, then for the purpose of proving the defence, the onus switches to the defence, who require to prove, on the balance of probabilities, that the accused was suffering from mental disorder or diminished responsibility when they committed the crime.

When a party bears the persuasive burden on an issue, the court must be satisfied on that issue to the required standard of proof, or the party will lose on that issue. The impact on the case as a whole depends on how central that issue is to the overall case.

Where the Crown have failed to discharge the persuasive burden at the close of the Crown case, i.e. to prove criminal responsibility of the accused beyond reasonable doubt, the defence may make a "no case to answer" submission. A "no case to answer" submission is in effect saying that, even if all of the evidence led by the Crown is accepted as proven by the trier of fact, i.e. either a judge or a jury, it would not amount to a sufficient case in law for a conviction. Of course, if a trial runs to conclusion that trier of fact may conclude that, as a result of cross examination or alternative evidence led by the defence, a reasonable doubt has been raised and the Crown have failed to discharge the persuasive burden and a verdict of not guilty should then follow.

The persuasive burden, in respect of proving or disproving guilt, does not transfer from the Crown at any stage. Suggestions to the contrary, for example, in *Fox v Paterson* (1948), that the effect of the doctrine of recent possession was to shift the onus of proof from the prosecution to the accused and to raise a presumption of guilt which the accused must rebut are wrong. The legal burden remains with the prosecution to prove the charge of theft or reset, but this can be discharged by proof of "recent possession" and the accused then bears the provisional or evidential burden if he is to avoid conviction.

THE EVIDENTIAL BURDEN

The evidential burden is the burden of adducing sufficient evidence on a particular issue to allow the court to begin considering it as a live issue. The party wishing to rely upon the evidence has the duty to lay down a basis for its proof.

This will arise in respect of an accused who pleads a defence. If the accused wishes to claim the defence of, for example, alibi, i.e. they were somewhere else when the crime was committed, they would be expected to lead some evidence to get their defence off the ground, for example, evidence of where they were on the particular date and time. It is important to note that the persuasive burden does not switch to the accused to prove the alibi, but there must be sufficient evidence presented to the court to allow the matter to be considered.

In general, there is no onus on the accused to prove a defence, in the sense of establishing it beyond reasonable doubt, or even on the balance of probabilities. The accused is subject only to an "evidential" burden—that is pointing to some evidence in the case in support of the defence which would entitle the jury to give the accused the benefit of the doubt.

WHO HAS THE EVIDENTIAL BURDEN?

Like the persuasive burden, the evidential burden is fixed by law and allocated to a particular party.

The default position is that on every issue both the persuasive and evidential burden is on the prosecution. The prosecution bear both burdens by default because of the presumption of innocence. As the presumption of innocence is a fundamental tenet of our criminal justice system, it follows that the burden of proof rests on the prosecution to displace this presumption, see *Mackenzie v HM Advocate* (1959). This default position will apply whether the issue to be proved emanates from common law or statute. Where a statute is concerned, any departure from the default position is a question of statutory interpretation in light of art.6(2) of the European Convention on Human Rights (hereinafter referred to as "the Convention").

DEVELOPMENT OF CRIMINAL LAW

Scottish criminal law is regarded by many as a flexible system as it is almost exclusively common law and is based on existing principles that have evolved through judicial decisions. It has neither a criminal code nor statutes in respect of the majority of crimes. But if we do not have a statutory system how do we create new crimes or amend existing crimes?

The High Court of Justiciary is regarded as having an "inherent power" to declare the common law. This power is called the "declaratory power". The declaratory power was described by Hume as the "inherent power to punish every act which is obviously of a criminal nature" (I, 12). This power is only exercisable by a quorum of at least three judges in the High Court of Justiciary. The last explicit use of the power was in *Bernard Greenhuff* (1838) when the accused was charged, along with three others, with keeping a public gaming-house. The accused objected to the relevancy of the indictment on the basis that the crime charged was not one known to the law of Scotland. Lord Justice Clerk Boyle said (at p.259):

> "I have looked into the authorities on this subject, and I have found enough to satisfy my mind, that there are solid principles in our law to justify a charge of this nature. It is of no consequence that the charge is now made for the first time."

He went on to refer to Hume and the power of the High Court to punish every act which is obviously of a criminal nature:

> "This court has a power to declare anything that has a tendency to corrupt public morals, and injure the interests of society, an indictable offence."

The plea to relevancy was refused. Lord Cockburn dissented in this case and his view, that the court's power was not to declare new crimes but to declare an existing crime committed in a new way, has been very influential.

There continues to be debate and conflicting opinion over whether the power was used in the last century. Many have argued that there are cases where the court has declared a new crime and that this is a de facto use of the declaratory power. Other commentators have viewed these cases as examples of an existing principle being applied to a new set of facts. The cases in this group generally involved a plea to the relevancy of the indictment or the complaint on the basis that no such crime exists and include: *Strathern v Seaforth* (1926) where it was held that "joyriding" amounts to the crime of clandestine use; *Kerr v Hill* (1936) where the court held that it was a crime to give false information to the police; *Watt v Annan* (1978) where organising the showing of a pornographic film in a private club was held to amount to shameless indecency; *Khaliq v HM Advocate* (1984) where the supply of glue-sniffing kits was held to amount to causing real injury; *HM Advocate v Wilson* (1984) where shutting off the electricity grid by pressing an emergency-stop button, resulting in economic loss rather than physical damage, was held to amount to malicious mischief; *S v HM Advocate* (1989) which established that a husband could be prosecuted for the rape of his wife with whom he was still cohabiting at the time of the alleged offence; and *Normand v Morrison* (1993) where it was held that letting police search a bag containing a contaminated needle amounted to reckless injury. In *Webster v Dominick* (2003), the decision of the court abolished the crime of shameless indecency, which was itself a judicial creation.

While there are no twentieth or twenty-first century cases where the power has been explicitly used, there are cases where the court has refused to create a new crime. In *Grant v Allan* (1987) the Appeal Court held that the clandestine taking of computer lists of customer information was not an offence known to Scots law and the complaint was dismissed. Lord Justice Clerk Ross and Lord McDonald acknowledged that to do otherwise would be creating a new crime and that this was the proper remit of Parliament.

The main objection to the declaratory power is based upon the principle of legality enshrined in Scots law. This principle expressed in the Latin maxim *nullem crimen sine lege* is that no one should be punished for an act that was not legally proscribed at the time of commission. The principle also requires that each crime should be capable of fairly precise definition so that its application to any particular set of facts can be clearly seen. Since the establishment of the Scottish Parliament in July 1999, under the authority of the Scotland Act 1998, neither the Parliament nor the Scottish Executive, which the Lord Advocate is a member of, can act in any way that is incompatible with the rights embodied in the Convention. The requirement for the criminal law and courts to comply with the Convention has so far predominantly affected procedural rather than substantive issues of criminal law. One area where there may be difficulties is in relation to the development of existing crimes or the introduction of new crimes as contravention of the principle of legality is also contravention of art.7(1) of the Convention, which states that:

> "No-one shall be held guilty of any criminal offence on account of an act or omission which did not constitute a criminal offence under national or international law at the time it was committed."

THE COURT STRUCTURE

A justice of the peace (not legally qualified) or a stipendiary magistrate (legally qualified) presides over a justice of the peace court ("JP court"). JP courts were created by the Criminal Proceedings etc. (Reform) (Scotland) Act 2007 and replaced the former district courts. The sentencing powers in this court are 60 days imprisonment (12 months if a stipendiary magistrate) or a fine not exceeding £2,500 (£10,000 if a stipendiary magistrate). Only summary trials are conducted in JP courts.

Summary and solemn trials are heard in the sheriff court as are fatal accident inquiries. In summary cases the maximum imprisonment is 12 months or a fine not exceeding £10,000. In solemn cases the maximum imprisonment is five years or an unlimited fine can be imposed.

The High Court of Justiciary will sit as a trial court, or court of first instance, for solemn trials only and has exclusive jurisdiction over treason, murder, rape and a breach of duty by magistrates as provided in the Criminal Procedure (Scotland) Act 1995 (hereafter the "CPSA 1995") s.3(6). This court can impose unlimited penalties. When sitting as an appeal court (Court of Criminal Appeal), the court consists of at least three judges in appeals against conviction and two judges for sentencing appeals. The number of judges sitting will mirror the complexity of the case before the court. The High Court will also hear cases referred to it by the Scottish Criminal Cases Review Commission. The High Court of Justiciary, sitting as an appeal court, is the final court of appeal in Scottish criminal cases except where a devolution issue is raised under the Scotland Act 1998. This provides that acts by the legislature or the executive that are contrary to the European Convention on Human Rights or European Community law can be appealed to the Supreme Court, although note some procedural changes have been introduced by the Scotland Act 2012.

READING

T. Jones and M. Christie, *Criminal Law*, 5th edn (Edinburgh: W. Green & Son, 2012), Chs 1 and 2.

C. Gane, C. Stoddart and J. Chalmers, *A Casebook on Scottish Criminal Law*, 4th edn (Edinburgh: W. Green & Son, 2009), Chs.1–3.

G.H. Gordon, *Criminal Law*, edited by M. Christie, 3rd edn (Edinburgh: W. Green & Son, 2000), Vol. I, Chs 1 and 2.

2. CRIMINAL RESPONSIBILITY

The definition of each common law crime is made up of a mental element (mens rea) and a physical element (actus reus). To understand both the content of substantive criminal law and also what is required to be proven for criminal responsibility to be established, both elements of each crime must be known. By approaching criminal law in this way, the student will grasp both the essential elements of criminal law and will appreciate the complexity and depth of the subject. It should be noted that all statutory crimes comprise a physical element, an actus reus, and some, but not all, have a mental element, a mens rea. Those crimes which do not have a requirement for a mental element are referred to as strict liability offences and are examined later in this chapter.

In addition to proving that the requisite mens rea and actus reus of a crime are present, it must also be shown that they coincide in time and, in respect of "result" crimes, that there is a causative link between the actions of the accused and the harm caused. These are the essential elements of criminal responsibility.

MENS REA

The basis of criminal responsibility is expressed in the Latin maxim, *actus non facit reum nisi mens sit rea*, which means (roughly translated) that the act cannot be guilty unless the mind is also guilty. Mens rea literally means "guilty mind".

One of the basic principles of legal and criminal responsibility is that those who are punished are those who deserve it, i.e. those who are considered to be morally or individually as well as factually responsible for what has been done. This is why proof of the mens rea, or mental element, of any crime is important as it will reveal whether the accused has committed the crime with the requisite mental element to be found criminally liable rather than having merely acted accidentally without the required mental state.

Before examining the different types of mens rea it is worth noting that the term mens rea is a relatively new one in Scots law and it was imported from English law. The term that preceded it, which also referred to the mental element of any crime, was "dole". Dole is derived from the Latin *dolus*, which is translated as "evil". Dole was defined by Hume as "that corrupt and evil intention, which is essential … to the guilt of any crime" (I, 21). The emphasis on evil, immorality and bad character are reflective of the historical period in which Hume was writing. As attitudes to criminal behaviour and offenders have changed over time, such moral condemnation for the character of the modern criminal are now restricted to the most serious crimes, e.g. murder and assault. The modern use and understanding of mens rea, as the mental element in crime, has become dominant in both common law and statutory crimes. Be aware, however, that continued reference to terms such as "wicked recklessness" in the crime of murder and "evil intention" in the crime of assault, indicate that the modern law has not yet completely abandoned history.

Proving mens rea

It is necessary to establish whether the test for mens rea is objective or subjective. An objective test is applied in Scots law (*Blane v HM Advocate* (1991)). A subjective approach to mens rea would require that the prosecution proves what the accused actually thought or had actually foreseen at the time of his actions. Clearly proving either of these things is impossible and, therefore, the courts adopt an objective approach which relies on what the accused should have thought or foreseen. Consequently, the accused will be judged by the standards of the reasonable person. The reasonable person test is merely an objective prediction of what the reasonable person should have thought or would have foreseen in the circumstances.

The use of an objective test allows the prosecution to prove the mens rea by inference from the evidence led, i.e. the actions of the accused and the other surrounding circumstances. In the case *Cawthorne v HM Advocate* (1968) Lord Justice Asquith stated (at p.33):

> "It is impossible ... to look into the mind of the man, and when, therefore, you are seeking to evaluate the effect of the evidence in regard to the nature and purposes of the act you can only do so by drawing an inference from what that man did in the background of all the facts of the case which you accept as proved."

In assessing the state of mind of an accused, evidence of events occurring before and after the crime was committed can be taken into account. In *McDowall v HM Advocate* (1998) the accused was charged with culpable homicide by driving a car in a culpable and reckless manner and with attempting to pervert the course of justice by failing to stop at the scene of an accident and failing to report that accident. The court held that the jury was entitled to consider the manner in which M had been driving prior to the accident in assessing his state of mind at the time of the accident and whether he had been showing a complete disregard for the possible consequences of his driving for the public.

In *Halliday v HM Advocate* (1998) two accused, A and P, were convicted of murder. At their trial they admitted killing the deceased and there was evidence that after the assault on the deceased they were seen shaking hands, saying that they were great brothers and then returning to the deceased and further assaulting him. After being told to stop, they placed the deceased in the recovery position and returned home where they attempted to wash their clothes. They later returned to the scene and called for an ambulance. At their trial the jury sought directions as to whether the wicked recklessness required for murder had to be at the same time of the assault or could include later events. A and P appealed against their convictions on the ground that the trial judge misdirected the jury to take account of all the surrounding events to the extent that they shed light on the nature of the assault and that the jury should have been told not to consider the handshake, the washing of clothes and the length of time taken to call an ambulance. The Appeal Court held, refusing the appeal, that evidence of events occurring after the attack was over were to be properly regarded as shedding light on the state of mind of A and P at the time of the attack and the fact that they had been wickedly indifferent to the consequences of their actions.

Mens rea and motive
Mens rea and motive are not the same thing. Motive is concerned with the reason an individual acted as she did. Although the motive of the accused may be important in terms of the evidence led at her trial and the punishment given, it is not considered when determining whether or not she is criminally responsible, e.g. to kill someone deliberately out of a humanitarian motive would still be murder. Similarly, claims that presenting an imitation handgun at a shop assistant and telling her to hand over money and lie on the floor was a joke did not serve as a defence in *Lord Advocate's Reference (No.2 of 1992)* (1992). The court held that the accused's assertion, that his actions were a joke, was only a statement of motive. He had acted deliberately and had the necessary intent for his actions to amount to assault and his motive was irrelevant.

Categories of mens rea
There are a number of *mentes reae*. There is a presumption that all common law crimes require mens rea. Intention and recklessness are the two main degrees of mens rea in common law and statutory crimes but other degrees including knowledge and wilfulness are also recognised. Most crimes will only have one mens rea but there are exceptions that have more than one, e.g. murder.

Intention
Intention suggests deliberate action and can be found in the definition of many crimes including murder (intent to kill), theft (intent to deprive), assault (evil intent) and fraud (fraudulent intent). While intending an action is a subjective state of mind, proving that state of mind involves an objective test. Case law notes that it is impossible to look into the mind of the accused and therefore an accused's "intention must, in the absence of any admission by him, be derived from the circumstances surrounding the incident" (*Carr v HM Advocate* (1995) at p.804B-C). It is not necessary to prove that the accused intended the consequence of his actions, e.g. a broken nose, rather, the mens rea of intention is inferred from the fact that a punch was thrown and it was deliberate. All of the proven facts of the case, the words and conduct of the accused and the circumstances surrounding the crime must be of a "sufficient quality to enable the

inference to be drawn of mens rea" (*Hughes v Crowe* (1993) at p.323).

The distinction between the mens rea of intention and recklessness has been blurred by references to a high degree of recklessness being equivalent to intention. In *Blane v HM Advocate* (1991) Lord Justice General Hope commented (at p.581F) that

> "since the matter must be approached objectively I think it is open to inference, where the accused is shown to have acted with a reckless disregard for the likely consequences of what he does, that he intended those consequences to occur."

Blane approved the direction to the jury in *HM Advocate v Boyd* (1977). In *Boyd* Lord Kincraig directed the jury that the necessary intention to set fire to the subjects could be implied from conduct indicating an utter disregard of the likelihood of the fire spreading to the subjects in question. In both cases, therefore, a high degree of recklessness was treated as being equivalent to intention. *Byrne v HM Advocate* (2000) overruled these earlier decisions. In *Byrne* (which involved a charge of wilful fire-raising) Lord Coulsfield notes (at p.91C) that the confusion in *Boyd* may have arisen from Lord Kincraig having in mind the crime of murder, which can be committed both intentionally and with wicked recklessness. Wilful fire-raising, however, only has one mens rea; namely intention. *Byrne* overruled *Blane* in so far as it approved the direction to the jury in *HM Advocate v Boyd* (1977). *Byrne* clarifies that in those crimes, where the mens rea is intention, a form of reckless mens rea, regardless of the degree, will not be adequate for intention to be inferred.

Transferred intention

Problems arise where the anticipated result of an accused's actions is affected by external circumstances. Examples include where A throws a glass intending to hit B and, as a result of being a poor aim, misses and hits C. The question which arises in these circumstances is can A be charged with assault when he intended to hit B but missed and hit C? The actus reus of assault is fulfilled but can the mens rea be transferred? Case law suggests that the mens rea can be transferred and this is described as "transferred intention". In *Roberts v Hamilton* (1989) Roberts was convicted at the sheriff court of assaulting Crawford and appealed to the High Court on the grounds that she lacked the requisite mens rea. The facts of the case were that Roberts had attempted to separate her cohabitee and her son who were fighting with each other. She intended to strike her cohabitee with a stick but missed and instead struck Crawford. The High Court refused the appeal, confirming the view of Hume, that criminal responsibility will arise where the accused has assaulted A in the belief that she is B, or alternatively A in error when she aimed at B (Hume, I, 22).

Subsequent decisions suggest that the doctrine of transferred intent only applies to the crime of assault and not to other crimes of intent, particularly, wilful fire-raising. In *Byrne v HM Advocate* (2000) a bench of five judges rejected the application of the doctrine of transferred intent in cases of wilful fire-raising. Like assault, this crime can only be committed intentionally. In *Byrne* the court held (at p.92) that

> "the jury may infer the necessary intention from all the relevant circumstances, but there is no room for the doctrine of transferred intent. Nor can any form of recklessness be treated as equivalent to intent ... before an accused can be convicted of wilful fire-raising in respect of any particular item of property in the charge, the Crown must establish that he intended to set fire to that item of property."

The judgment of the court did not refer to *Roberts v Hamilton*. However, if such an approach was adopted, it would appear that a charge of assault could not succeed and conviction would only follow if an alternative charge of reckless injury had been libelled.

Recklessness

Criminal recklessness was defined as "a total indifference to and disregard for the safety of the public" in *RHW v HM Advocate* (1982) at p.420. Recklessness is determined by an objective test and does not require that the accused was aware of, or considered, the possible risks from his behaviour (which would amount to a subjective test being applied, see *Allan v Patterson* (1980)). Reliance on the subjective test used in *Allan v Patterson* (1980) has subsequently been described as "problematic" in *Carr v HM Advocate* (1995), *Thomson v HM Advocate* (1995) and *Cameron v Maguire* (1999), which have reinforced that an objective test should be employed. An objective test results in the actions of the accused being considered against those of the "reasonable person" and the question is whether those actions demonstrate a total indifference to and disregard of what the consequences of the act in question may be so far as the public are concerned. The use of such an objective test underlines that an accused is assumed to have some awareness of risk when carrying out a criminal or legal act.

In homicide two forms of recklessness are recognised. In the crime of murder the mens rea includes wicked recklessness and in culpable homicide the mens rea is recklessness. These are examined in more depth in Ch.3.

Knowledge

The mens rea of knowledge is required in some crimes, e.g. in reset or in the crime of assaulting a police officer. In both instances the accused must know or reasonably suspect the status of either the goods in question or the individual. Evidence of actual conscious knowledge on the part of the accused may not be necessary if the evidence suggests that the accused ignored the obvious. In the case of *Latta v Herron* (1967) the accused appealed against conviction of the reset of two guns. The sheriff at first instance had accepted that the accused was not conscious that the guns he had purchased were stolen but said that the full circumstances of whom they were purchased from and where this took place, etc. raised an inescapable inference that they were dishonestly obtained and the accused had "wilfully blinded himself to the obvious". The Appeal Court confirmed the finding of the sheriff and the appeal was dismissed.

Negligence

Negligence involves risk-taking or lack of care of a degree greater than would be expected of the "reasonable person". While this is similar to recklessness, they are differentiated by the degree of risk-taking or carelessness. Common law does not regard merely negligent behaviour as criminal. In some statutory offences, however, negligence would be adequate mens rea to constitute criminal liability, e.g. careless driving.

Error and absence of mens rea

Error is relevant in two contexts. First, where the accused, as a result of the error, lacks the necessary mens rea for the crime charged. Secondly, error can also result in the accused believing that his intentional actions were justifiable.

Absence of mens rea

The first category of error is where, as a result of error, the accused lacks the necessary mens rea for the crime charged. In these circumstances, she cannot be held responsible for the crime. This scenario would arise where, e.g. an accused takes a shopping bag in the belief that it is her own, therefore lacking the intention to deprive another of that property (which would be necessary for the crime of theft). However, such errors of judgement do not always serve to negate criminal responsibility, namely where the error is reckless. In such a scenario, although the accused may lack the necessary intention to commit a crime, her reckless mental state may fulfil the mens rea requirement of certain crimes. This is illustrated in respect of the crime of rape which has a mens rea of intention or recklessness. It has been held that if an accused has recklessly formed a belief that the woman is consenting to intercourse and she is not, this reckless error will not serve as a defence (*Jamieson v HM Advocate* (1994)).

An error occurring in the commission of a crime will not serve to negate criminal responsibility if the essential ingredients of mens rea and actus reus are still present. For example, in the case of *Andrew Ewart* (1828) the accused and his victim were guarding a graveyard. The accused mistook his companion for a body snatcher, and shot and killed him. He was charged and convicted of murder, since it would have been murder if he had killed an actual body snatcher.

Intentional actions and error

The second category of error is relevant when the accused acts intentionally but in the belief that her actions are justifiable. Here the nature of the error is significant in relation to whether or not it will be deemed to be acceptable in law. There are two types of error in this group: (a) errors of law and (b) errors of fact. Errors, which arise through mere ignorance of the law, are not recognised. As a matter of public policy people are presumed to know the law. Factual errors may be recognised if they fulfil certain criteria.

(a) Error of law. In *Clark v Syme* (1957) the respondent was charged with maliciously shooting and killing a neighbour's sheep. His defence was that he thought his actions were legal because he had forewarned his neighbour that sheep were damaging his crops and that he would shoot any animals that wandered onto his land. His defence of error of law was accepted at trial and he was acquitted. The prosecutor appealed by way of stated case to the High Court. Lord Justice General Clyde said (at p.5):

> "[T]he mere fact that his criminal act was performed under a misconception of what legal remedies he might otherwise have had, does not make it any less criminal".

On some occasions an error of law can serve to negate the mens rea of a crime. This would apply where an accused takes property in the erroneous belief that it belongs to her. In these circumstances, the accused will lack the intention to deprive the owner of their property, which is the mens rea of theft. This is called an erroneous claim of right and can act as a defence to a charge of theft. Such a defence is not available where an accused takes property, never believing it to belong to her, but in the belief that it is not criminal to do so. The question of erroneous claim of right was raised in *Dewar v HM Advocate* (1945).

In *Dewar* the appellant, a crematorium manager, had been convicted of the theft of two coffins and a number of coffin lids. He appealed against conviction and sentence. At trial his defence was that he mistakenly believed that, following their delivery to him, he was entitled to dispose of the coffins and coffin lids as he wished, and that this was the common practice at other crematoria. During his evidence Dewar conceded that his belief as to the practice at other crematoria was wrong and there was insufficient evidence to support his belief. Lord Justice General Normand said (at pp.11–12):

> "[T]he presiding judge took a lenient view when he instructed the jury to consider whether the appellant might have entertained an honest and reasonable belief, based on colourable grounds, that he was entitled to treat the coffins as 'scrap'. The presiding judge pointed out that the jury must not exculpate the appellant merely because he entertained an erroneous belief founded on some singular notions of his own, but that they must discover some evidence that he had rational and colourable grounds for believing that he was entitled to remove, retain and dispose of the coffin lids."

The Appeal Court refused the appeal, finding that the direction by the trial judge was not only fair but lenient to the accused. Lord Justice General Normand indicated that the defence of error was irrelevant in *Dewar* as there was adequate evidence upon which the jury was able to convict of theft. It is significant that Dewar did not believe the coffins were his property but, in the knowledge that they belonged to someone else, thought that he could dispose of them as he wished.

(b) Error of fact. An error of fact can serve to justify an accused's actions if it is both honest and reasonable. In *Owens v HM Advocate* (1946) the accused wrongly believed his attacker had a knife and was about to kill him and so he killed the attacker in self-defence. He was convicted and, on appeal, the conviction was quashed due to the fact that the jury had been misdirected at the trial on the question of self-defence. The opinion of the court was that, if the jury had come to the conclusion that the appellant genuinely believed that he was gravely threatened by a man armed with a knife but the deceased actually had no knife in his hand, it would have been their duty to acquit and the jury ought to have been so directed. The actions of an accused must be both honest and reasonable if an error of fact is to serve to justify the accused's actions.

The requirement that a factual error be both honest and reasonable is accepted as now applying to all crimes including rape where belief in the victim's consent must be honest and reasonable (Sexual Offences (Scotland) Act 2009 s.1(1)(b)).

STRICT LIABILITY OFFENCES

Strict liability offences occur where there is no need to prove a mental element. Although this type of liability is found only in statutory offences, most statutory offences will conform to the usual rule that mens rea must be proven before there will be a conviction, e.g. *Sweet v Parsley* (1970) and *H v Griffiths* (2009). The onus is on the Crown to show that an offence is one of strict liability (*Duguid v Fraser* (1942)). Strict liability offences are more commonly found in regulatory offences, e.g. speeding offences in road traffic legislation (*mala prohibita*) rather than offences that cause harm (*mala in se*), e.g. sexual offences in the Sexual Offences (Scotland) Act 2009.

ACTUS REUS

The term actus reus has no official or accepted meaning but is generally used to denote the behavioural element of a crime. Actus reus includes the conduct, omission or situation which, if accompanied by an appropriate mens rea, would result in criminal responsibility. Criminal responsibility, for the most part, depends on the performance of overt acts. A criminal or anti-social thought is not enough to lead to a conviction.

In conduct crimes, the actus reus is the conduct required. For example, in assault it is "any attack upon the person of another which causes fear or alarm". In result crimes, the actus reus is the conduct which brings about the result. For example, in murder the actus reus is "a wilful act causing the destruction of human life". The law does not classify different methods of taking life as individual actus reus. It is the taking of life rather than the mode of doing so that is relevant.

It is necessary that the accused voluntarily brought about the wrong that has occurred. In most cases this requirement is clearly fulfilled. However, there are occasions when the accused is not deemed to have acted voluntarily either because things occurred outwith her control or where she had a lack of control over her own actions. Where an accused has carried out a criminal act, without this essential self-control, no criminal responsibility will attach. Examples of this can be seen in cases where the harm caused was a result of bad weather as in *Hogg v Macpherson* (1928); where the accused's actions were deemed to be a "reflex" response (see *Jessop v Johnstone* (1991)); or where another had physically compelled the accused to act as they did (see *HM Advocate v Hugh Mitchell* (1856)).

There is no definitive list of actus reus of common law crimes. Rather, each crime has a particular actus reus. Whereas statutory offences narrate the relevant actus reus in the section of the statute, the actus reus of common law crimes is found by consulting the works of the institutional writers and court decisions. Both common law and statutory offences sometimes require a number of different types of conduct for the actus reus. For example, the common law crime of uttering as genuine requires both a forged document and the presentation of it as genuine to another person. In *George Skene Edwards* (1827) a jury returned a verdict of guilty of forgery alone on a charge of "uttering as genuine". The conviction was quashed on appeal as "forgery" was not a known crime. If an accused person has completed only some of the essential steps towards fulfilment of the actus reus of a crime, she may be convicted of an attempt to commit that crime.

Although there is no definitive list of actus reus of common law crimes, it is useful to classify actus reus into three groups:

(1)   an overt or positive act;
(2)   an omission; and
(3)   a state of affairs.

(1) An overt or positive act

It is generally assumed that all actions are overt or positive. Whilst such actions may involve a physical movement of the body, an overt or positive act can also refer to types of conduct. As noted above, such an overt or positive act is assumed to be voluntary. Actions that are shown to have been induced by an external factor, over which the accused has no control, will generally not be regarded as criminal.

(2) An omission

Omissions do not generally attract criminal responsibility in Scots common law. In a small number of statutes criminal responsibility will arise where the accused fails to do something. For example, s.172 of the Road Traffic Act 1988 requires the owner or keeper of a vehicle to give information to the police as to the identity of the driver of that vehicle at a material time. This requirement was held not to be a breach of the Convention in *Jardine v Crowe* (1999). This type of offence is described as a *crime of omission* and is generally distinguished from crimes of *commission committed by means of omission*.

In respect of the common law, there is no assumption of the Good Samaritan and, therefore, an individual who finds another in peril is not legally obliged to intervene and assist that person. There are certain situations, however, where such intervention is legally required and failure to intervene will result in criminal liability. Crimes of commission committed by means of omission include:

(a)   where the omission follows a prior dangerous act;
(b)   where the accused's status or contractual obligations result in a duty to act; or
(c)   where there is a prior relationship between the accused and the victim which is such that there is a legal obligation to act.

(a) Where the omission follows a prior dangerous act. In this type of situation the accused's omission generally follows a prior positive act. The prior positive act may be criminal or not criminal.

In *HM Advocate v McPhee* (1935) the accused was charged with murder. The indictment alleged that he had assaulted a woman, compressed her throat with his hands, beat her with his fists, knocked her to the ground and kicked her repeatedly, and "did expose her in the said field while in an injured and unconscious condition to the inclemency of the weather". The accused lodged a preliminary plea to the relevancy of the charge that was repelled by the court. Lord Mackay stated (at p.50) that there could be a murder conviction if it was proved that the accused "wickedly and feloniously exposed the unconscious woman regardless of consequences to the inclemency of the weather, and if she died in consequence ... both of the beating and the exposure". At trial, the accused was convicted of culpable homicide.

In cases of this sort, if it can be proven that the accused's initial criminal actions caused the victim's death, the question of omission will not arise. However, where the accused's initial criminal action has weakened the condition of the victim, the accused has a responsibility to either remove the victim or obtain help to aid them in the dangerous situation he has created.

The situation becomes more complicated where the initial actions of the accused are not criminal but merely accidental or negligent, but their subsequent actions cause a harm which may be regarded as criminal so long as they amount to the crime charged. In *McPhail v Clark* (1983) a fire deliberately set to burn straw spread to the adjacent roadside and the resultant smoke created a dangerous situation for motorists and a number of vehicles crashed. The farmer was convicted of recklessly endangering the lieges. His action of allowing the fire to spread and doing nothing about it for at least 20 minutes, when it was assumed he must have seen what was happening, was held by the sheriff to demonstrate a reckless indifference to the consequences for the public generally and for the particular road users directly affected by his actions.

McPhail v Clark can be distinguished from *McCue v Currie* (2004) as in the former case the actions of the accused amounted to the crime charged, namely reckless endangerment, whereas in *McCue v Currie* the actions of the accused were not sufficient for a charge of culpable and reckless fire raising. In *McCue* the appellant was charged that he "culpably and recklessly set fire to a caravan and the fire took effect thereon". He entered the caravan to commit theft and was using a lighter to see his way around. He accidentally dropped the lighter which, due to a defect, did not extinguish when it hit the floor. He was aware he had started a fire but did nothing to extinguish it or to summon help. At the trial the sheriff accepted that the appellant had accidentally dropped the lighter. He convicted the appellant on the basis that his act was not just unintentionally dropping the lighter but also his complete disregard for the obvious consequences of doing nothing thereafter. His conviction was quashed on appeal. The High Court held that: (1) culpable and reckless fire raising cannot be committed solely by the fact that the person was engaged in an illegal act when the fire was started; (2) the mens rea of recklessness in a case of culpable and reckless fire raising is determined by the state of mind of the perpetrator when the fire is started and not his state of mind thereafter; (3) the drafting of the charge in this case referred to culpability and recklessness at the point the fire was started and thereby the prosecutor was offering to prove that the dropping of the lighter was reckless rather than accidental; and (4) that fire raising which is merely accidental is not a crime and cannot become so on account of subsequent behaviour on the part of the person concerned. The court stated that the failure of the appellant to take steps after the fire started was reprehensible and that there may be a case for enacting a new crime of culpably failing to take appropriate steps after a situation of danger to persons or property has arisen as a result of a person's actions, but that this was not a matter for the court.

(b) Where the accused's status or contractual obligations result in a duty to act. This would apply to people in public office or a position of responsibility. Liability would arise in this situation where the individual had a duty to prevent the occurrence of harm and fails to discharge the duties imposed by his position. In the case of *Bonar and Hogg v MacLeod* (1983) the accused (a police officer) failed to intervene to prevent the assault of a person in police custody by an officer junior to himself. He was regarded as art and part liable for the said assault. In *William Hardie* (1847) Hardie was a Poor Law inspector who was convicted of culpable homicide when death resulted from his failure to deal with an application for assistance. Liability will arise where the accused fails to discharge the duties imposed by his position.

(c) Where there is a prior special relationship between the accused and the victim which is such that there is a legal obligation to act. Although the idea of the Good Samaritan or "being your brother's keeper" is generally not embraced in Scots criminal law, it is assumed that a legal obligation to protect will exist in relationships between, e.g. a parent and a minor child. This obligation to protect is not, however, absolute and it is clear from the decision in *Bone v HM Advocate* (2005) that personal characteristics of the accused will be taken into account in assessing whether parental actions and omissions are reasonable. In *Bone* B was convicted of the culpable homicide of her daughter by witnessing and countenancing criminal conduct towards her by B's co-accused (her partner). B appealed arguing that: (1) her parental responsibility towards her daughter did not involve criminal responsibility for the failure to protect the child or to intervene in the assault being perpetrated by her co-accused where she was powerless to intervene; (2) there was insufficient evidence to entitle the jury to find that she had "countenanced" the murder; and (3) that the judge failed to direct the jury that they should take account of her subjective characteristics, notably her limited ability to react and her particular vulnerability as stated in the evidence of the forensic psychologist, when they were assessing what was reasonable in respect of the alleged failure to protect her daughter. The court held that: (1) there had been a material misdirection regarding the evidence which was relevant to the question of whether B had taken reasonable steps to protect the child and ensure her wellbeing; and (2) the jury should have been given guidance as to what circumstances might properly have been regarded as relevant to the reasonableness of B's acting and omissions and, in particular, regard should have been had to B's physical and psychological condition in deciding whether she acted reasonably as well as deciding the question of diminished responsibility.

A legal obligation to protect or act would not, however, be assumed to pertain to all other relationships. If a relationship of dependence does arise, however, a legal obligation to protect or act may follow, e.g. an obligation to protect could arise where a householder has a long-term lodger who is gravely ill. Failure to summon medical assistance in these circumstances may result in criminal responsibility. In the English case *R. v Instan* (1893) the accused lived with her aged aunt whom she neglected by not giving her any food for 10 days and failed to obtain medical help to deal with the gangrene her aunt had developed. As a result, the aunt died and the accused was convicted of manslaughter. Both the family relationship and, more importantly, the relationship of dependence between the two parties resulted in the niece having a legal obligation to protect. While there is no reported case law on this specific point in Scotland it is assumed that *Instan* would be followed.

Is there a duty to prevent the commission of a crime?

There is no Scottish authority to the effect that a person who fails to take steps to prevent a crime does thereby commit an offence. In *HM Advocate v Kerr* (1871) one of the three men accused of assault with intent to ravish had not participated in the assault but had watched from the adjoining field. The jury were directed that they should not convict the accused in the absence of evidence that he had encouraged the others by language or presence.

(3) A state of affairs

The third type of actus reus is a state of affairs. This will normally be found in statutory offences. For example, s.4(2) of the Road Traffic Act 1988 provides that a person who, when in charge of a mechanically propelled vehicle which is on a road or other public place, is unfit to drive through drink or drugs, is guilty of an offence. However, it also appears in the common law crime of breach of the peace. The Appeal Court in *Smith (P) v Donnelly* (2001) held that the actus reus of breach of the peace required conduct severe enough to cause alarm to ordinary people and threaten serious disturbance to the community.

CONCURRENCE OF ACTUS REUS AND MENS REA

The actus reus and mens rea must coincide in time if criminal liability is to be established. Generally, the mens rea would be expected to proceed or occur contemporaneously with the actus reus. In *Thabo v R* (1954) the appellants were convicted of the murder of a man, whom they had assaulted and, believing that he was dead, thrown his body off a cliff. Medical evidence showed that the man had not been dead but that he did later die from exposure. The attempt by the appellants to argue that the mens rea and actus reus did not coincide in time was unsuccessful and the court held that they could not divide up what was a series of acts.

VICARIOUS LIABILITY

Vicarious liability occurs where one individual is held responsible for the actions of another. Vicarious liability is not recognised in respect of common law crimes and is presumed not to exist in relation to statutory crimes unless otherwise specified. Vicarious liability offences are found in the CJLSA 2010 s.141(B), where the licence holder or an interested party may be held liable for the actions of an employee or agent.

CORPORATE LIABILITY

The prosecution of companies for strict liability offences is unproblematic.

If mens rea is required to be proven, however, prosecution and conviction for certain crimes will be more difficult. The difficulties encountered in charging a company with murder or culpable homicide are illustrated by *Transco Plc v HM Advocate* (2004), where the court held that a charge of culpable homicide against Transco Plc was irrelevant. The Crown accepted that it could not identify any particular natural person in that company capable of being characterised as its directing mind and will, and also the necessary guilty mind. The court rejected the Crown's suggestion that the "committees and posts" referred to in the indictment could replace such a person. The company was convicted of health and safety offences. The difficulties encountered by the prosecution in this cause undoubtedly influenced the Crown's decision to charge ICL Plastics and their subsidiary ICL Tech only with health and safety offences following the *Stockline* explosion as this avoided the thorny issue of proving mens rea (*ICL Plastics Ltd v Scottish Ministers* (2005)). The companies pled guilty to four breaches of health and safety legislation and were each fined £200,000. The difficulty of proving mens rea whilst bringing a charge which states that someone has been killed will be avoided in future by relying on the offence of corporate homicide.

The offence of corporate homicide has been introduced by the Corporate Manslaughter and Corporate Homicide Act 2007. Section 1 of this Act makes it an offence for a relevant organisation (a corporation, a departmental body, a police force or a partnership, trade union or employer's association, that is an employer) to manage or organise its activities in a way that causes a person's death and amounts to a gross breach of a relevant duty of care owed by the organisation to the deceased. If convicted of an offence under this legislation, the punishment is an unlimited fine. Where in the same proceedings, a charge of corporate homicide and a health and safety offence have arisen out of all or some of the same circumstances, it shall be competent to convict of both.

In crimes involving dishonesty it may be possible to prove the requisite directing mind and therefore mens rea, e.g. *Purcell Meats Ltd v McLeod* (1987) where it was confirmed on appeal that a company could be guilty of fraud.

CAUSATION

Criminal responsibility for result crimes requires proof of the mens rea, the actus reus and causation. Causation requires that the actions of the accused caused the harm suffered. In many cases causation is straightforward, e.g. in an assault where the accused has punched the victim on her nose, it is obvious that the accused has caused the harm suffered. The situation becomes more complicated, however, where an accused has carried out a wrongful act, e.g. a serious assault and thereafter complications with medical treatment occur and the victim dies. To find an accused guilty of murder or culpable homicide in these circumstances one must be satisfied that there is a direct causal link between the unlawful act, in this scenario the assault, and the victim's death. To establish a causal link, the "but for" or *sine qua non* test must be satisfied. This test is "but for the actions of the accused would the victim have died?", i.e. were the actions of the accused "a substantial and operating and continuing cause of death" (*Finlayson v HM Advocate* (1979)). If it is accepted that the accused's actions contributed significantly to the victim's death, i.e. an operating and substantial cause, then one must go on to consider whether the causal link is direct or indirect. Some actions may pass the "but for" test but be deemed to be too remote in time or circumstance to be direct causes of death. An intervening event which breaks the chain of causation is known as a novus actus interveniens.

Causation requires to be established for every result crime, i.e. those crimes which require a resultant harm, but it tends to be most problematic in respect of the crimes of murder and culpable homicide. The importance of demonstrating the accused's responsibility for a death where there are intervening or pre-existing factors is obvious. In testing whether the necessary causative link exists, the characteristics of the victim, the conduct of the victim, the intervention of third parties (e.g. medical treatment) and the reasonable foreseeability of the outcome will be considered. These are guiding legal principles rather than strict legal rules. These guiding principles are examined below.

Characteristics of the victim

This is also known as "taking your victim as you find him" or the "thin skull" rule. This principle is commonly considered in the situation where a victim with a pre-existing medical condition is attacked and death results. The general approach adopted by the courts has been that the accused must take responsibility for his actions even where the victim has a pre-existing medical condition.

In *HM Advocate v Robertson and Donoghue* (1945) the accused were charged with assault, robbery and murder. The case against the first accused was that he had assaulted an elderly shopkeeper, struggled with him and inflicted certain slight injuries on him. Medical evidence disclosed that the deceased had a very weak heart and that the elderly man died of heart failure. Robertson was found guilty of culpable homicide; the case against Donoghue was not proven. In his summing up, Lord Justice Clerk Cooper said:

> "[I]t is none the less homicide to accelerate or precipitate the death of an ailing person than it is to cut down a healthy man who might have lived for fifty years."

In *Hendry v HM Advocate* (1987) the accused was convicted of culpable homicide. He had been charged with assaulting a 67-year-old man by punching, knocking him down and kicking him, in consequence whereof he suffered a heart attack and died. Medical evidence disclosed that the deceased suffered from heart disease, other stressful factors were present, and one doctor stated in evidence that he could only say on the balance of probabilities that the assault had caused the heart attack. The accused appealed against his conviction on the basis that the evidence at trial had revealed a number of possible factors which could have triggered the heart attack which occurred 15 to 20 minutes after the assault. Counsel for the appellant submitted that none of these factors had been established to such a standard as to entitle the trial judge to direct the jury that they could be satisfied beyond reasonable doubt that the assault had caused the death of the deceased. He maintained that, at best, the jury might have been able to take the view on a balance of probabilities that the heart attack had been caused by the assault. The court held that the question of whether a causal link between the assault and the death was established beyond reasonable doubt was a matter for the jury and there was sufficient evidence to entitle the jury to discount the other stressful factors and to be satisfied on that question, and the appeal was refused. This approach was confirmed in *McDade v HM Advocate* (2012) where the appellant was charged with having punched the deceased on the head, struggled with him, caused him to fall downstairs and repeatedly struck him with a knife, all to his severe injury and, in consequence, the deceased had suffered a fatal heart attack. The jury convicted of culpable homicide under deletion of the violence libelled except repeated stabbing. There was evidence that the stabbing was one factor in a matrix of stressors, including the distress caused by the situation and the underlying health complaints, that put the deceased at risk of a heart attack at any time. The court held, rejecting the appeal, that it was a matter for the jury to decide whether the elements of the attack found by them to be criminal had made a significant contribution to the onset of the heart attack. The court referred to Lord Reed in *Johnston v HM Advocate* (2009), at para.[56], where he said "Whether [a] causal connection has been established in a particular set of circumstances is a question to be determined by the jury, applying ... their common sense".

The question of causation is more complex where the commission of the crime committed is not witnessed by a victim who subsequently dies from a pre-existing medical condition. In *Lourie v HM Advocate* (1988) two accused were charged with the culpable homicide of a 74-year-old woman in that they entered her home uninvited and stole her handbag in her presence, and as a consequence she sustained a fatal heart attack having previously suffered from heart disease. Both accused were convicted at trial and appealed on the ground that, in the absence of any violence or intimidation directed against the deceased, there could be no culpable homicide. The Appeal Court held that, in the absence of evidence to prove beyond reasonable doubt that the accused had "entered the house uninvited and there in her presence steal a handbag", the conviction of culpable homicide could not stand. Convictions of theft of the deceased's handbag were recorded against both appellants. This case suggests that a conviction of culpable homicide in circumstances involving not violence but another unlawful act requires, at least, that the unlawful act must be carried out in the presence of the deceased and most probably be directed at her or her property. It is not enough for the victim to die when she later discovers the unlawful act has been carried out.

The characteristics of the deceased have also been recognised as including, e.g. religious beliefs, as is illustrated by the English case *R. v Blaue* (1975). The accused was charged with the murder of a young woman by stabbing her. The woman had been taken to hospital where she had refused a blood transfusion because she was a Jehovah's Witness. She did not receive a transfusion and died four hours later. It was accepted that she would have survived if she had accepted the transfusion. The accused was convicted of manslaughter on the basis of diminished responsibility and appealed against conviction. The appeal was dismissed and Lord Justice Lawton said (at p.450):

> "The physical cause of death in this case was the bleeding into the pleural cavity arising from the penetration of the lung. This had not been brought about by any decision made by the deceased girl but by the stab wound."

This case is persuasive authority that both the physical and psychological characteristics of the victim must be taken as found by the perpetrator of a crime.

Conduct of the victim
Even in situations where the voluntary actions of the victim have contributed to the harm suffered, this has not served to break the chain of causation. Examples of this are found where an accused is held responsible for supplying noxious substances that the victim voluntarily ingests, where the victim does not mitigate the effects of injuries inflicted and where the victim deliberately harms himself.

Noxious substances
The position in Scots law is that an accused who recklessly supplies noxious substances will be held responsible for any harm resulting if their voluntary ingestion by the victim was reasonably foreseeable. This relates to substances that are themselves legal and illegal. In *MacAngus v HM Advocate* (2009) a bench of five judges considered the issue of causation where an accused supplies a noxious substance which the recipient then voluntarily ingests. The court followed the previous Scottish authorities which held in the case of *Khaliq v HM Advocate* (1984) that, depending on the circumstances of the case, supply could be regarded as equivalent to administration and therefore could be taken as a cause of injury and, in the case of *McDonald v HM Advocate* (2007), that, if the victim acted in a wholly unforeseeable or unreasonable way, that would break the chain of causation. In deciding this, it is the foreseeability of the actions rather than the outcome that is important. The court further held that a charge libelling culpable homicide in the context of supplying or administering a controlled

drug was relevant only if the Crown offered to prove that it was done recklessly and that the perception following the *Lord Advocate's Reference (No.1 of 1994)* (1995), that the commission of an unlawful act causing death, without proof of recklessness, could amount to culpable homicide was incorrect.

Victims and mitigation of harm

Victims are generally not assumed to be responsible for mitigating the harm they have suffered unless they have "reacted in a wholly unforeseeable or unreasonable way that would mean that the attack would cease to be a direct cause of the death and thus the requisite causal link would not be established" (*McDonald v HM Advocate* (2007) at p.16, para.[11]). In such circumstances, the actions of the victim could be deemed to amount to a novus actus interveniens and consequently break the chain of causation (*R. v Williams and Davis* (1992)). The question of victim responsibility for mitigating harm can arise in a number of contexts, including where the victim is fatally injured when trying to escape an attack. Case law suggests that, in these circumstances, the accused will be held responsible for the death of the victim. In *Patrick Slaven* (1885) a woman was attacked by the accused who intended to rape her. When she attempted to escape the accused pursued her and she fell over a cliff and died. The accused's conduct was held to be the cause of the woman's death. In *McDonald* the appeal court approved the trial judge's three stage causation test, namely: first, "but for" the conduct of the accused would the victim have died; secondly, was the cause direct or indirect; and thirdly, whether the victim acted in a wholly unforeseeable or unreasonable way that would mean that the attack would cease to be a direct cause of death and the causative link would be broken. As noted above, the victim's responsibility has been considered in respect of those who supply noxious substances and their subsequent responsibility should the recipient be harmed or die as a result of voluntary ingestion.

The time lapse between the actions of the accused and the response by the victim is relevant in cases where the victim is fatally injured escaping an attack. In *McDonald v HM Advocate* (2007) the appellant and a man, B, were convicted of culpable homicide as a result of having assaulted the deceased and causing him to fall from a window. The assault, which took place in the deceased's third floor flat, was not disputed. There was evidence that, when the assailants left the flat, B locked the door and took the key. Some time not later than 30 minutes after the appellant and B left, the deceased climbed out of his kitchen window, apparently in order to reach the street. The lintel of a window on the second floor, however, broke when he stood on it and he fell to the ground and died as a result. There was no evidence that the deceased tried to leave by the door or that he knew it was locked. There was no telephone in the flat. The deceased, who was a drug addict, had consumed a considerable quantity of amphetamine. The court held that the attack had ended a short time, between 5 and 30 minutes, before the victim climbed out of the window. In light of the shortness of that interval and the evidence of the victim's fall, it was open to the jury to infer that he was trying to escape and that the attempt was prompted by the attack. Therefore, it was not essential for the Crown to prove that the victim knew the door had been locked. The appeal was refused. The court distinguished *Broadley (Rose) v HM Advocate* (2005) where the accused had successfully appealed against a culpable homicide conviction. There the time lapse between the acts alleged to have been committed by the accused, namely assault and abduction and the deceased's action in climbing out of the window, was in excess of 24 hours and, as there was no evidence of the accused having even been in the room at or shortly before the fall from the window, the conviction was quashed.

The question of mitigation of harm may also arise where the victim of an assault does not follow medical advice and subsequently dies. In the case *Jos. and Mary Norris* (1886) the two accused were charged with the culpable homicide of a man whom they had assaulted. None of the wounds inflicted had been serious and the victim received prompt medical treatment. However, the man had died eight days later from tetanus. There was evidence that the man had ignored medical advice, drunk alcohol and removed his own bandages. Lord Craighill directed the jury that, if they believed the tetanus was brought on by the deceased's actions rather than the attack, the accused were entitled to be acquitted. However, if their belief was that the tetanus had been caused by the attack and would have developed regardless of how the accused had behaved, then the verdict would have to be one of guilty. The jury returned a verdict of "not proven". The direction to the jury in this case has been regarded as somewhat unusual and as having been influenced by the unfavourable view of alcohol abuse adopted by the law. It is generally assumed that an accused will be responsible for the consequences of their actions regardless of how the victim has behaved after the harm has been inflicted. The test is whether a substantial and operating cause of death is the actions of the accused and the resultant injuries.

Victims who deliberately harm themselves
If the victim of an assault deliberately self-harms and accelerates her death, the perpetrator of the original assault may still be held responsible for her death. This would be dependent upon whether the actions of the accused were deemed to be a cause of death.

There is no Scots case law on this point. In the US case *People v Lewis* (1899) the accused shot his victim in the stomach and then put him to bed. A few minutes later the victim cut his throat. Medical evidence suggested that the gun-shot wound would have caused death within one hour and the cut throat caused death within five minutes. The accused was convicted of manslaughter and unsuccessfully appealed. His actions were deemed to have contributed to the victim's death and the throat cutting did not serve to break the chain of causation.

Intervening causes

Proof of causation becomes more complex where there are intervening events between the actions of the accused and the death of the victim. It is unusual for an intervening event to break the chain of causation unless it is truly independent of the harm caused by the accused. An intervening event which does break the chain of causation is known as a *novus actus interveniens*. Case law demonstrates that courts are reluctant to recognise intervening causes as breaking the chain of causation. The effects of intervening causes will be examined under three headings: assault and subsequent infection, inadequate medical treatment and other medical intervention.

Assault and subsequent infection

In general, the law will not recognise external intervening causes as breaking the chain of causation unless they prove to be a wholly unpredictable cause of death. Therefore, in those cases where a victim of a serious assault develops a wound infection and dies this would not break the chain of causation (see *James Wilson* (1838)). However, if the victim of a non-fatal assault were to contract an illness while in hospital and die as a result of that illness, this would most probably be seen to be a new and unpredictable cause of death unrelated to the actions of the accused. This is illustrated by the US case *Bush v Commonwealth* (1880) where the victim had suffered a gun-shot wound and thereafter died from scarlet fever while in hospital. It was held that his death was as a result of contracting the disease and not the original assault. Both this case and that of *James Wilson* (1838) emphasise that, before a subsequent infection will be treated as a *novus actus interveniens*, it must be independent of the original injury.

Inadequate medical treatment

Inadequate medical treatment is also known as *malregimen*. Where the injury or wound is serious, intervening poor medical treatment will not break the chain of causation and the perpetrator will be held responsible for the resulting death. However, if the wound or injury is so minor that, without the poor medical treatment it would not have caused death, the poor medical treatment will serve as a *novus actus interveniens* (*James Williamson* (1866)). The question is, therefore, one of foreseeability and whether it was foreseeable that the actions of the accused would cause the death of the victim.

Other medical intervention

The impact of other medical intervention would arise, e.g. where an assault victim's life-support machine is turned off. In *Finlayson v HM Advocate* (1979) the victim had suffered brain death following the injection of a controlled drug. The High Court held that turning off the life-support machine was foreseeable and did not break the chain of causation. The effects of the injection were held to be the substantial and continuing cause of death.

ART AND PART LIABILITY

Art and part liability, sometimes referred to as "acting in concert", arises where two or more individuals participate in the commission of a crime. This participation can be the result of a common plan or purpose, or can arise spontaneously. Art and part liability applies to both common law and statutory offences. Whilst the criminal law will generally only hold an accused responsible for their individual actions, where a common purpose, i.e. art and part liability can be established, the accused will be held responsible for the actions of others within the group. This may appear unreasonable if an individual has only offered minor assistance, e.g. as a "lookout" in a bank robbery. Although the different levels of participation will not affect criminal responsibility they will, however, be taken into account at the point of sentencing. Conversely, if a number of people are involved in a criminal incident but no common purpose, either planned or spontaneous, can be shown, then each will be judged only on the basis of their own actions. In such a scenario, where more than one accused has inflicted injuries on the victim but the jury conclude that the deceased had been killed by only one of the accused, but were unable to decide which, then in the absence of proof of common purpose, either planned or spontaneous, all accused must be acquitted (*Johnston v HM Advocate* (2009)).

Participation and degrees of involvement
Art and part guilt can result from different types of participation in a criminal purpose. These include the provision of material assistance prior to the commission of the crime and physical assistance at the time of commission of the crime. Art and part liability will also apply to situations where an offence is committed at the instigation of someone else. Therefore, where an assassin is hired, both the assassin and the hirer will be held art and part liable for any crime that is committed as part of the common plan.

Mere presence at the scene of a crime will not result in art and part responsibility if the accused was not part of a common plan to commit a crime, did not engage with others spontaneously to commit a crime and did not encourage the commission of the crime or intimidate the victim (*George Kerr and Others* (1871)). However, presence accompanied by minimal activity will be enough to constitute art and part responsibility where there is a common criminal purpose. In *Vogan v HM Advocate* (2003) the appellant was present when a number of men burst into the complainer's flat and attacked him. The appellant was described by the complainer as having been present but just "raking about the house" and standing speaking. The appellant's conviction for attempted murder was upheld because although he had not inflicted any wounds on the complainer he was acting with others in pursuance of the common criminal purpose of assaulting the complainer.

Counsel or instigation

Counsel or instigation refers to the situation where advice is given in respect of the commission of a crime or where the perpetrator's commission of a crime is instigated by others. In both scenarios, where there is a common plan, all parties involved will be held responsible for the commission of the crime. Where a group of individuals conspire to commit a crime, their agreement is enough for them to be charged art and part with conspiracy. General advice will not constitute either counsel or instigation (Hume, I, 278). Any counsel or instigation must be given before the crime is carried out. In *Martin v Hamilton* (1989) a solicitor was charged with contravening s.176 of the Road Traffic Act 1972, which makes it an offence to aid, abet, counsel, procure or incite another person to commit an offence against the provisions of that Act. The charge was held to be irrelevant as the client had failed to report a road traffic accident at the first opportunity and, therefore, had already committed the crime by the time he allegedly saw the solicitor and was advised not to report the accident.

Provision of material assistance

Prior to art and part guilt being established on the basis of material assistance, it must be shown that the parties have participated in a common plan to commit a crime. If this can be shown, the level of assistance provided is irrelevant in establishing criminal responsibility. However, any assistance must have been provided prior to the commission of the crime. Although the provider of assistance need not be aware of every aspect of the crime planned or have participated in the commission of the crime, it is clear that they must be aware that they are assisting a criminal purpose. There must also be some connection between the actual perpetrator of the harm and the assistance provider.

In *HM Advocate v Johnstone and Stewart* (1926) the two accused were charged with procuring an abortion while acting in concert. The two women had never met. Johnstone had obtained Stewart's name from a third party and had passed this on to persons interested in obtaining an abortion. Lord Moncrieff directed the jury that if they accepted the evidence that the women were strangers and that no money was paid by Stewart to Johnstone for the referral, then art and part guilt could not be established. Johnstone was acquitted and Stewart convicted.

Assistance at the commission of the crime

Common Plan. *HM Advocate v Lappen* (1956) provides a good example of art and part guilt arising from a common plan. In this case, the accused and five others were charged with assault and robbery. Lord Patrick directed the jury (at p.110):

> "[I]f a number of men form a common plan whereby some are to commit the actual seizure of the property, and some according to the plan are to keep watch, and some according to the plan are to help to carry away the loot, and some according to the plan are to help to

dispose of the loot, then, although the actual robbery may only have been committed by one or two of them, every one is guilty of the robbery because they joined together in a common plan to commit the robbery."

The leading modern authority on art and part guilt is *McKinnon v HM Advocate* (2003). In *McKinnon* a bench of five judges held that an accused is guilty of murder art and part where, first by his conduct—for example, actions or words—he actively associates himself with a common plan which is or includes the taking of human life or carries the obvious risk that human life will be taken and secondly, in carrying out that purpose, murder is committed by someone else. The court stressed that it is a decision for the jury whether an accused should be held responsible for murder when he knew that a weapon which could readily be used to kill was being carried for use in furtherance of a criminal purpose, so that there was an obvious risk of murder, and that in such a situation it would be immaterial whether he knowingly ran that risk or was recklessly blind to it. This decision confirms that the question of foreseeability is one that is to be assessed objectively, i.e. the test is what was reasonably foreseeable to those who participated in the attack.

Spontaneous common purpose. A spontaneous common purpose is most likely to be found in relation to crimes of violence. One would not expect, e.g. a group of people to spontaneously decide to rob a bank and obviously this type of crime is more likely to be planned or at least openly agreed to in advance. In *Gallacher v HM Advocate* (1951) three accused were part of a larger group who stood around a man and kicked him to death. There was no evidence that this attack was planned or that there had been prior agreement. The spontaneous attack on the man was viewed as the common purpose and all three were convicted of murder.

Distinguishing between co-accused

In cases of concert, where a number of accused have been involved in assaulting the deceased it is often not possible on pathological grounds alone to differentiate between the injuries produced by a punch or a kick. In such a scenario the jury must consider whether the assault carried out by each accused is a contributory cause of death. In *Malone v HM Advocate* (1988) death was caused by multiple blows to the head and it was not possible to distinguish between any specific blow or blows. The two appellants had assaulted the deceased in concert, then one had stopped while the other continued to inflict further blows. The court rejected a submission that the appellant who bore no responsibility for the final blows could not be convicted of the killing, holding that since he bore responsibility for the earlier blows delivered in concert, and those blows could be considered to have materially contributed to death, he had been properly convicted and the appeal was refused. *Malone v HM Advocate* (1988) and *Melvin v HM Advocate* (1984) provide authority that it is legitimate for the culpability of multiple accused who have killed another to be assessed separately so long as there is neither antecedent nor spontaneous concert. This may result in one (or more) accused being convicted of murder and the other(s) being convicted of culpable homicide. This should only occur where the evidence permits the jury to differentiate the relative degree of recklessness attributable to each accused resulting in some being assessed as having a mens rea of wicked recklessness (murder) and others a mens rea of recklessness (culpable homicide). In such circumstances, the judge must direct the jury as to the circumstances in which a verdict of culpable homicide would be open to them if intending to convict a co-accused of murder (*Hopkinson v HM Advocate* (2009)). Such a scenario will not arise where a common plan has been established which included the taking of human life or carried the obvious risk that human life would be taken (*Melvin v HM Advocate* (1984) at pp.366–367; *McKinnon v HM Advocate* (2003)). In a case involving a joint assault causing death, the responsibility of co-accused could only be distinguished if there were striking differences in the relevant conduct of each of the parties (*Melvin v HM Advocate*).

In the case of spontaneous concert, where a weapon is used by only one of the accused, other accused can only be found guilty on an art and part basis if there is sufficient evidence to prove that he actively associated himself with the attack in the knowledge that the weapon was being, or was liable to be used in the course of it. Where such an attack involves the use of a normally harmless item as a weapon, it will be more difficult to prove that an accused had knowledge that such an item was being or would be used as a weapon. In *Herity v HM Advocate* (2009) the appellants were charged with assaulting the victim with a golf club. The incident took place on a pitch and putt course when the appellants approached the complainer and his brother and asked if they could play with them. On being refused one of the appellants picked up one of the complainer's golf clubs and started hitting a ball. The other appellant then picked up another golf club and started hitting a ball. The identification of which accused had struck the complainer was not corroborated and, therefore, the only basis for convicting either of the accused was that they had acted in concert. The court held that if there was concert it was spontaneous. Given that the assault involved the use of a weapon, the appellant who did not wield the golf club could only be convicted on an art and part basis if there was sufficient evidence to prove that he actively associated himself with the attack in the knowledge that the club was being, or was liable to be, used in the course of it. The court further stated that in cases such as this, particular care was required where, as here, there was nothing untoward about the use of a golf club on a pitch and putt course and part of the unpleasantness towards the complainer and his brother consisted of taking their clubs and pretending to play with them. As directions to that effect had been lacking in the sheriff's charge to the jury this amounted to a miscarriage of justice as there was a risk that without appropriate directions that the jury might convict the appellant who did not wield the club on the basis of his mere presence. The appeals were allowed and the convictions quashed.

Unforeseen consequences

Lappen provides a relatively straightforward example of art and part guilt. However, this becomes more complex when things are done that are not part of the common plan. It must then be decided if all partners to the common plan are responsible for this unforeseen incident or whether the perpetrator should be held solely responsible. For example, if a group of individuals agree to rob a bank and have fake guns and one of the group produces a real gun and shoots the teller dead, should all of the group be held responsible for this death? When deciding this question the courts have focused on whether the unplanned actions were reasonably foreseeable. If they are, all of the group will be held responsible.

The approach adopted in recent cases including *Boyne v HM Advocate* (1980) and *Codona v HM Advocate* (1996) indicate that the blanket responsibility that was once assumed to accompany evidence of a common plan is now more fragile. Individual responsibility is now more closely examined, including the foresight, mens rea and participation of each accused.

In *Boyne v HM Advocate* (1980) three accused were charged and convicted of murder. The victim had been stabbed with a knife and there was evidence that this was not part of the common plan. The Lord Justice Clerk found that there was nothing to show that the two appellants knew or had reasonable cause to believe that the actual killer would use a knife on the victim. There appears to have been evidence that one of them knew that the killer sometimes carried a knife, but it appears that he believed that it was for self-defence and had never seen him use the knife in previous assaults. As an alternative ground of responsibility, the judge considered that if either co-accused had carried on with the assault after they saw the knife being used this would have made them art and part guilty. The murder convictions of the two accused who did not have the knife were quashed and verdicts of guilty of robbery and assault substituted.

In *Codona* the appellant, a 14-year-old girl, had been convicted art and part of murder and appealed to the High Court on the ground that there was insufficient evidence of guilt, art and part in the murder, and on the ground that her statement to the police was inadmissible, having been unfairly obtained. The murder conviction resulted from her participation in an assault which resulted in the death of the victim. Earlier that evening she had participated in two other assaults on men who were robbed. Although each of these assaults had involved the use of weapons, neither involved murderous violence of the type used in the final assault. The appellant had admitted kicking the deceased on the foot at the start of the attack. Evidence from blood stains on her clothing suggested she was near the deceased when he was punched while still standing. The court held that there was inadequate evidence to entitle the jury to convict the appellant of murder. Even if her statements were deemed admissible, the court held that, when the appellant had kicked the deceased at the start of the attack, there was no indication that she had reason to think that she was participating in a murderous attack. The court also held that the appellant's statements that she kicked the deceased once on the foot at the start of the assault ought not to have been held to be admissible. The conviction was quashed.

The suggestion in *Brown v HM Advocate* (1993) that the prosecution had to prove the accused had foreseen the use of a weapon by their co-accused and that the requisite mens rea of murder would accompany its use has been rejected in *McKinnon v HM Advocate* (2003). *McKinnon* confirmed that an objective test (reasonable foreseeability) is used to assess the guilt of those acting in concert. In *Poole v HM Advocate* (2009) the court confirmed that the test in such cases is whether there was evidence entitling the jury to find that it was objectively foreseeable to the appellant that such violence was liable to be used as carried an obvious risk of life being taken. The same test also applies when non-fatal violence is used. In *Shepherd v HM Advocate* (2009) the appellant was convicted of robbery art and part. The complainer gave evidence of being woken at 1am and finding two men in his home. One of the men assaulted him whilst the appellant asked him where his property was and ransacked the flat. The appellant appealed on the basis that there was no corroboration of robbery as distinct from theft and no evidence of concerted enterprise involving violence. The court rejected the appeal stating that, when domestic premises are broken into in the middle of the night, it must be in the contemplation of the parties to that enterprise that violence may be required and used against the occupant who must be expected to be there.

The question of forseeability becomes more complex where, e.g. the carrying of some weapons forms part of the common plan but the fatal violence is done with a different weapon. In *O'Connell v HM Advocate* (1987) four accused were convicted of murder. There was evidence that the common plan had involved the accused carrying sticks to use in their attack on the victim. However, a hammer belonging to the victim had been used to strike the fatal blow. The trial judge directed the jury that, if the four accused formed a common plan to assault the victim with weapons that were capable of causing death or serious injury, or were aware that such weapons were likely to be used, then, if in the course of that assault someone used another weapon which was of a similar type and capable of inflicting similar injury, then all of the parties involved would be equally guilty as the man who inflicted the fatal blow. It was left to the jury to decide if a hammer was the same type of weapon as a stick. This direction was approved on appeal and the conviction confirmed. The liability of co-accused in such a scenario where a gun was used instead of sticks is less certain. However, this direction confirms that it would be for the jury to decide whether weapons are similar in respect of their capacity to inflict injury.

Where there are unintended consequences and the common purpose has arisen spontaneously, the test of forseeability is also used. In these circumstances, however, where there is not a common plan, the accused are more likely to be judged solely on their own actions. In *Dempsey v HM Advocate* (2005) the appellant and F were charged art and part with the murder of the deceased by striking him with a knife. The murder happened during a dispute the appellant and F had with the deceased, the final phase of which started with the appellant striking the deceased with a cooking pot, knocking him down and pinning him to the floor, and ended when the appellant got up off the deceased. F admitted he had stabbed the deceased repeatedly. The appellant denied that he had struck the deceased with a knife, stated that he had not seen a knife being used and was only aware of blood when he got up from the deceased. The court held that in these circumstances, where it was alleged that there was spontaneous concert, the appellant could have been convicted of murder only if the jury were satisfied that he knew that F had the knife and was using it on the deceased, and that, with that knowledge, he had continued with the joint attack on the deceased. The court held that the trial judge had misdirected the jury that a conviction was possible if they were satisfied that the appellant could have known that F had a knife and was using it, even if it could not be inferred from the evidence that he did know these facts.

Participation in an ongoing offence or after the offence has been committed
This situation is most likely to arise in respect of crimes of violence where, for example, the accused joins an individual or a group who are already assaulting the victim. *McLaughlan v HM Advocate* (1991) suggests that, if criminal activity is already under way when the accused participates, then his criminal responsibility will only extend to the acts committed after his participation. He cannot be held responsible for any actions carried out before he participated. However, in *Kabalu v HM Advocate* (1999) the court held that, as there was insufficient evidence to entitle the jury to hold that the appellant must have witnessed extreme and fatal violence on the deceased prior to him delivering one or two kicks, there was insufficient evidence to convict of murder. As a result, his murder conviction was quashed and a conviction of assault was substituted. The decision of the court suggests that witnessing extreme and fatal violence prior to participating, with minor violence, in an on-going assault, could result in a murder conviction. Accession after the fact is not a doctrine recognised by Scots law and the suggestion of the court in *Kabalu* may have resulted from the fact that the accused in this case had admitted to being party to a common plan with the co-accused to assault the deceased.

As accession after the fact is not recognised in Scotland, assistance or participation following the commission of a crime does not result in criminal responsibility for that crime. Assisting with the disposal of the stolen "getaway car" that has been used for a robbery will not, therefore, result in the helper being art and part guilty of robbery unless this was planned in advance of the robbery and was, therefore, part of the common plan. If no such plan existed and the hiding of the car was only agreed after the robbery, the helper may be charged with reset (the retention of stolen goods), which is a separate offence.

Acquittal of co-accused

A charge of art and part guilt can arise where all of the accused are principal offenders and also where only one or some of the accused are principal offenders and the others are accomplices. Where all of the accused are principal offenders it is possible for some to be convicted and others acquitted, e.g. *Capuano v HM Advocate* (1984). Similarly, where there are principal and accomplice offenders it is possible for the principal to be convicted and the accomplice acquitted. Where, however, the crime is such that the participation of the principal offender is necessary for the commission of the offence and they have been acquitted, their accomplice will not be convicted. In *Young v HM Advocate* (1932) Young and his co-accused, who were the directors and company secretary of a limited company, were charged with the fraudulent allotment of shares in that company. Young was convicted and his co-accused acquitted. On appeal his conviction was quashed because only people in the position of his co-accused could deal in the shares of the company. As they had been acquitted and he could not have acted on his own, his conviction was quashed.

Until recently it was assumed that the trial of one accused could not take place following the trial and acquittal of their co-accused, e.g. *McAuley v HM Advocate* (1946). However, this has now been overruled by *Howitt v HM Advocate; Duffy v HM Advocate* (2000).

Omission and art and part liability

Art and part liability can arise from a criminal omission, but only in those limited circumstances whereby a sole offender would be responsible for a criminal omission. The question of art and part responsibility for an omission tends to arise in circumstances where the co-accused is present during, but does not participate in, the commission of a crime. As there is no duty to prevent the commission of a crime in Scots law, this scenario does not generally lead to art and part guilt. However, in limited circumstances including where a co-accused is in a position of authority, criminal responsibility may arise from a failure to act. In *Bonar and Hogg v MacLeod* (1983) the accused, a senior police officer, failed to intervene to prevent the assault of a prisoner in police custody by an officer junior to himself. He was found to be art and part responsible for the assault. The common purpose presumably arose spontaneously here when the senior officer watched the junior officer assault the prisoner.

Outwith these special categories, where responsibility for criminal omissions arise, there will be no art and part guilt if an accused is merely present at the commission of a crime. In *HM Advocate v Kerr* (1871) three accused were charged with assault with intent to ravish. One of the accused, Donald, had not participated in the assault but had watched from the other side of a hedge in an adjoining field. Donald objected to the relevancy of the charge against him. Lord Ardmillan rejected the plea to the relevancy and ruled that the charge should go to the jury in order that all the circumstances be disclosed in evidence. He stated (at p.337) that:

"It may be, that Donald actually encouraged the other prisoners by his language, or by his presence ... as to indicate readiness to give assistance, not to the girl but to her assailants, if necessary, and thus intimidating the girl."

Lord Ardmillan directed the jury that as Donald was not in the field, but only looking through the hedge, it would not be safe to convict him.

Withdrawal from the common plan
The criminal responsibility of someone who withdraws from a common plan will depend on whether the accused withdraws at the preparation or perpetration stage. There are two conflicting public policy views on this. An individual should be able to change his mind once he has decided to embark on a criminal course but this must be balanced with the fact that a person cannot escape criminal liability when he had ensured that a crime took place by participating in its early stages, and had then left to avoid the consequences.

If there is withdrawal after the crime has started then the accused will not escape criminal liability. In *MacNeil v HM Advocate* (1986) eight people were accused of drug smuggling by transporting drugs on board a ship from Nigeria to the UK. The appellant and another accused left the ship when it arrived at a Spanish port. The appeal court differentiated between an accused who abandons a crime which is at the stage of preparation and one at the stage of perpetration. The Lord Justice General (at p.318) said:

"If a crime is merely in contemplation and preparations for it are being made, a participator who then quits the enterprise cannot be held to act in concert with those who may go on to commit the crime because there will be no evidence that he played any part in its commission. If, on the other hand, the perpetration of a planned crime or offence has begun, a participant cannot escape liability for the completed crime by withdrawing before it has been completed unless, perhaps, he also takes steps to prevent its completion."

The appeal was dismissed and the court emphasised that there was no defence of dissociation in Scots law. It is not clear from this judgment what lengths an accomplice would have to go to in order to prevent the completion of a crime; however, it should involve contacting the authorities.

INCHOATE CRIMES

Inchoate crimes are crimes where the actus reus has not been completed. Although criminal intention alone is never punished, it is not necessary that a crime be completed before the activity falls within prohibited behaviour. There are three specific crimes which deal with situations where the criminal activity falls short of a completed crime and these are known as inchoate crimes, they are: attempt, conspiracy and incitement.

ATTEMPT

All crimes may be attempted and any attempt to commit a crime is itself criminal (CPSA 1995 s.294). Why does the law penalise attempts? There are a number of possible reasons, including the criminal has clearly done her best to commit a crime but has been prevented from doing so by some external factor. This wickedness is viewed as being something that should be punished for both retributive and deterrence purposes.

An attempted crime comprises an actus reus and a mens rea. The mens rea will be identical to that of a completed crime. This is straightforward where the mens rea of the completed crime is intention, e.g. theft. However, problems arise when the mens rea of a crime is recklessness. Generally, Scots law does not recognise the possibility of a reckless attempt, as an essential part of the crime of attempt is that the accused intended to commit the crime which is libelled. The exception to this general rule is the law relating to attempted murder. In *McGregor v HM Advocate* (1973) at p.56 Lord Keith charged the jury as follows:

> "If you go out and recklessly fire off a firearm or wave a knife or dagger about and kill somebody, that may be murder. The test of attempted murder is whether, if the actions of the accused had resulted in the death of one of the [complainers] you would have said that was murder or not. If a man drives along with a policeman on his bonnet in such a way that the policeman falls off and is killed ... if you would have said that was murder, then you would be entitled to convict him [of attempted murder]."

Actus reus
Whilst the mens rea of attempted crimes is relatively straightforward, a more difficult issue is the actus reus. Even if a crime is not completed, an accused can be said to have the requisite mental state for the mens rea of that crime. If the actus reus is not completed, however, it is necessary to determine the point at which the accused's activities become an attempt to commit a crime. When does a non-criminal preparation become an attempt at a crime? Intention alone is not enough, there must also be some conduct on the part of the accused which constitutes the crime and provides evidence of intention. No exact point in the perpetration of a crime has been identified in case law as amounting to the actus reus of an attempted crime. It is clear that merely forming the mental intention to commit a crime without further action is not enough (*HM Advocate v MacKenzies* (1913)). Apart from this, however, case law is inconsistent and centres around three theories, although it is not always clear which is being employed by the courts. There is evidence that the third of these theories has been preferred

in more recent cases. The three theories are:

(1)   irrevocability theory;
(2)   last act theory; and
(3)   perpetration theory.

(1) Irrevocability theory

This theory suggests that a criminal attempt requires that the effect of the accused's actions must be irrevocable. In *HM Advocate v Tannahill and Neilson* (1943) a partner in a firm of contractors was charged with attempting to induce sub-contractors, who had done work for him, to invoice a government department for this work, thereby attempting to defraud the government department. Lord Wark charged the jury that, as there was no evidence of any overt act on the part of the accused the consequences of which they could not recall, the jury were not entitled to convict of attempt to defraud. A verdict of not guilty was returned.

This approach results in criminal responsibility not arising until very late in the perpetration of a crime. It is obvious that, if such an approach was universally adopted, this would produce difficulties for law enforcement and may also allow individuals to avoid criminal responsibility merely because of a chance intervention in their plans. More recent cases do not require that the situation has become irrevocable before criminal responsibility will arise.

(2) Last act theory

This theory is based on the idea that criminal liability for attempt will arise when the accused has done all that he believes is necessary to commit the proposed crime.

In the case of *Samuel Tumbelson* (1863) the accused was charged with attempting to poison his wife by giving a quantity of poisoned oatmeal to an innocent third party to give to his wife. An objection was taken to the relevancy of the indictment on the grounds that there was no averment that the poisoned oatmeal had reached or had been eaten by the woman or that the poisoned oatmeal had been placed beyond the control of the accused. Lord Neaves (at p.430) said:

> "With regard to the second objection, it is true that the mere resolution to commit a crime is not indictable ... but when, as in the present case, machinery is put in motion, which, by its own nature is calculated to terminate in murder—when this agency is let out of the party's hands to work its natural results—that is a stage of the operation by which he shows that he has completely developed in his own mind a murderous purpose, and has done all that in him lay to accomplish it."

The approach adopted in *Samuel Tumbelson* contradicts the first theory and, despite the early date of the case, adopts a stricter interpretation of the actus reus of attempt than is utilised in *HM Advocate v Tannahill and*

Neilson (1943). If the last act theory is adopted it would result in criminal responsibility not arising until a fairly advanced stage of perpetration has been reached and this is no doubt why it is not the preferred approach in recent Scottish cases.

(3) Perpetration theory

This third theory places a more onerous burden upon an accused, as it recognises a more flexible approach to the actus reus of attempt than the previous two theories. Perpetration theory is based on the premise that attempt involves any move, however slight, from preparation to perpetration. This appears to be the preferred approach in Scots law.

In *HM Advocate v Cameron* (1911) a husband and wife were charged with the attempted fraud of an insurance company. They had insured a necklace as their own property although they only had temporary possession of it, staged a fake robbery and intimated this to their insurance broker. At their trial, the prosecution failed to prove that an insurance claim had been made although there was evidence of a letter by the accused to their insurance broker detailing the robbery. When directing the jury Lord Justice General Dunedin (at p.485) said that the essential question was where preparation ends and perpetration begins. He noted that this was a question of degree and it was a question that should be decided by the jury. He went on to say:

> "The mere conceiving of the scheme—if you think a scheme was conceived—is not enough; but if that scheme is so carried out as that a false insurance is taken, and that a false robbery is gone through, very little more will do. At the same time you must remember that the actual claim has not been made."

The direction emphasised that the jury had to consider whether the actions of the accused had gone beyond the stage of preparation into the stage of perpetration. Both accused were found guilty.

The test of moving from preparation to perpetration was also adopted in the subsequent case of *Barrett v Allan* (1986), where a drunk man in a turnstile queue at a sports ground ignored the police warning not to enter the ground and instead returned to the queue a few minutes later. On being arrested he said "I'm no that drunk. I'm going in". In *McKenzie v HM Advocate* (1988), the Appeal Court confirmed that the approach adopted by the sheriff, namely, that the test is whether the accused had passed from the stage of forming the fraudulent scheme and had set it in motion by overt acts, was the correct one. This approach is clearly the most effective from a crime prevention and control perspective. However, it is not unproblematic. It is accepted that it is difficult for juries to determine when an accused has moved from mere preparation to the perpetration of a crime. This theory does provide a workable law of criminal attempts and perhaps a more precise definition of attempt is both impossible and impractical. This is illustrated by the fact that other jurisdictions apply an equally vague definition of attempt.

Attempting to do the impossible

Attempting the impossible includes such scenarios as attempting to steal from a pocket that is empty. In this situation the accused intends to carry out a particular crime and is prevented from doing so by some chance element. There was conflicting case law on this point until the decision in *Docherty v Brown* (1996). Prior to *Docherty* an accused was convicted of attempted theft from an empty pocket in *Lamont v Strathern* (1933). This decision conflicted with the approach by the courts in two cases, *HM Advocate v Anderson* (1928) and *HM Advocate v Semple* (1937), which each involved an accused charged with attempting to procure an abortion by supplying drugs to a woman who was believed to be pregnant. In each case the accused was acquitted as the recipient was not pregnant. Clearly, the approach of the court in *Lamont* conflicted with that in *Anderson* and *Semple*. The five bench decision in *Docherty v Brown* (1996) has clarified that, in Scots law, impossibility does not act as a defence to a charge of attempt.

In *Docherty* the appellant had been convicted of possession of drugs with intent to supply, contrary to the Misuse of Drugs Act 1971. The appellant had mistakenly believed that the tablets in his possession contained a controlled drug. This was incorrect and the tablets were in fact harmless. The appeal was refused. The account of the law by Lord Justice Clerk Ross received the support of three of the other judges. He noted (at p.60) that:

> "For a relevant charge of an attempt to commit a crime, it must be averred that the accused had the necessary mens rea, and that he has done some positive act towards executing his purpose, that is to say that he has done something which amounts to perpetration rather than mere preparation. If what is libelled is an attempt to commit a crime which is impossible of achievement, impossibility is irrelevant except that there can be no attempt to commit the crime if the accused is aware that what he is trying to do is impossible."

This decision clarified that the previous distinction between legal and factual impossibility is no longer an issue in impossible attempts. However, where an accused mistakenly attempts an action which they believe to be criminal but it is in fact legal, no criminal responsibility will arise.

CONSPIRACY

A conspiracy requires the intentional agreement of two or more people to commit a crime (*Maxwell v HM Advocate* (1980)). The mens rea of this offence is intention and the actus reus is agreement to commit a crime. Nothing else needs to be done in pursuance of that agreement for a crime to have been committed. However, it will be difficult to prove a conspiracy unless there is evidence indicating that such an agreement was reached

(*Sayers v HM Advocate* (1981)). A conspiracy charge may libel that specific crimes were carried out in pursuance of the conspiracy, but where the indictment is more vague and merely refers to a conspiracy to achieve a purpose by criminal means, it is necessary that the criminal means be specified or the charge will be held to be irrelevant (*Sayers v HM Advocate* (1981)).

While individuals are often charged, both with conspiring to commit a crime and the completed crime, it is not competent to convict an accused of both. The reasons for charging both include that it allows evidence relating to events leading up to the commission of the crime to be considered by the court and also that it increases the chances of conviction, as it may be easier to prove a conspiracy to commit a crime rather than the completed crime. An objection to the competency of charging both conspiracy to murder and murder was made in a preliminary diet of the Lockerbie trial (*HM Advocate v Al Megrahi* (2000)). This preliminary plea was refused by Lord Sutherland (at p.189 D–F).

Proving conspiracy

In conspiracy cases it is unlikely that a witness will be available who can speak to agreement being reached between the accused. As a consequence, evidence of a conspiracy will be inferred from the actions of the accused. In *West v HM Advocate* (1985) the accused were charged with conspiring to assault and rob employees who worked in a particular building. The charge narrated that, in furtherance of the conspiracy, the accused

> "[did] loiter in the vicinity of said premises ... and thereafter enter the said premises while ... in possession of a blade from a pair of scissors, and ... in possession of an open razor, all with intent to assault said employees with said weapons and rob them of money."

On appeal it was held that there was sufficient evidence from which to infer a conspiracy.

Conspiring to do the impossible

The approach adopted by the courts to conspiring to do the impossible mirrors that adopted in relation to impossible attempts. As noted above, the crime of conspiracy is committed when two individuals agree to commit a crime and, therefore, the fact that some intervening event would make the completion of the crime impossible is irrelevant. In *Maxwell v HM Advocate* (1980) Lord Cameron directed that, since conspiracy involved the agreement to achieve a criminal purpose, it was the criminality of that agreement and not the result which makes the activity criminal. Impossibility is, therefore, irrelevant.

Withdrawal as a defence?

Where two individuals have agreed to a criminal purpose, they have committed the crime of conspiracy. As a result, at the point of agreement the crime of conspiracy is complete and there is no opportunity to withdraw. It would be possible for an accused to have abandoned the criminal purpose at a later point. This may affect her responsibility for either the attempted crime or the completed crime, but she would still have conspired to commit the crime.

INCITEMENT

A person who invites another to participate in the commission of a crime is guilty of incitement. The crime is committed as soon as the invitation is made and is not dependent on the invitation being accepted. Indeed, if the invitation is accepted, the crime would then be one of conspiracy rather than incitement. The mens rea of incitement is the intention that the incited party commit the relevant crime and the actus reus is the invitation. The use of social networking sites as a means of inciting others is evident in case law, for example, in *Divin v HM Advocate* (2012), where the accused pled guilty to incitement as a result of posting Facebook messages which encouraged individuals to riot in Dundee at a time when there was widespread civil unrest in London.

INCITEMENT, CONSPIRACY AND ART AND PART GUILT

Each of the above are potentially stages in the commission of a crime where more than one person is involved. Incitement involves one person inviting another to participate in a criminal purpose. If this invitation is accepted, then at that point, the two (or more) parties are described as conspiring to commit the crime. If either or both go on to attempt or commit the crime, then they will be regarded as art and part liable in the commission of the crime, due to their common plan.

READING

T. Jones and M. Christie, *Criminal Law*, 5th edn (Edinburgh: W. Green & Son, 2012), Chs 3, 5, 6 and 7.

C. Gane, C. Stoddart and J. Chalmers, *A Casebook on Scottish Criminal Law*, 4th edn (Edinburgh: W. Green & Son, 2009), Chs 2–6.

G.H. Gordon, *Criminal Law*, edited by M. Christie, 3rd edn (Edinburgh: W. Green & Son, 2000), Vol. I, Chs 3–9.

3. CRIMES AGAINST THE PERSON

NON SEXUAL OFFENCES AGAINST THE PERSON

ASSAULT

The crime of assault can be described as an intentional attack upon the person of another. The actus reus of assault is an attack upon the person of another and the mens rea is evil intention.

Actus reus of assault

The actus reus of assault has been interpreted widely by the courts and has been held to include attacks which do not result in injury, indirect attacks and even words where no violence is used. The use of physical violence in the course of a "fight" is probably closest to the popular understanding of assault. While this would amount to an assault, other types of behaviour are also included in the definition.

What constitutes an assault? Case law indicates that any degree of violence that is deliberate fulfils the legal definition of assault, e.g. putting paper in someone's hand and setting fire to it (*Lachlan Brown* (1842)) or twisting someone's hand behind their back (*Codona v Cardle* (1989)). Harm does not require to be caused to the victim and, therefore, aimed blows or missiles which miss the intended victim may still be held to constitute an assault (*Stewart v Procurator Fiscal of Forfarshire* (1829)).

Does an assault require to be direct? An assault may not even involve direct contact between the accused and the victim. In *Quinn v Lees* (1994) the accused was charged with setting his dog on three boys by giving the dog the command "fetch". The accused claimed that this was done as a joke. As the dog was held to be unable to distinguish between a command and a joke, the accused was held to have carried out a deliberate act with predictable consequences.

Can a person be assaulted on the basis of gestures? An assault can also be committed by making threatening gestures that place the victim in a state of fear and alarm. In *Atkinson v HM Advocate* (1987) the Appeal Court confirmed a conviction of assault in respect of the appellant who had entered a shop wearing a face mask and jumped over the counter to where the cashier was standing. The Appeal Court held that an assault may be constituted by threatening gestures that are sufficient to produce alarm.

The mens rea of assault

Assault is a crime of intent in Scots law and, therefore, cannot be committed recklessly or negligently. The mens rea of assault was described by Macdonald as "evil intent" (Macdonald, *A Practical Treatise on the Criminal Law of Scotland*, 5th edn (1948)). The definition of "evil intent" was, until recently, expressed as "intent to injure and do bodily harm" (see Lord Justice General Wheatley in *Smart v HM Advocate* (1975) at p.33).

The definition of "evil intent" has been clarified in the leading modern authority on the question, *Lord Advocate's Reference (No.2 of 1992)* (1992). In this case the accused was charged with assault with attempt to rob and attempted robbery. He had entered a shop, pointed an imitation gun towards the owner and asked for the contents of the till. When he realised that there were other people in the shop, the accused ran out. In his evidence the accused said that his actions were a joke. The jury were directed that if they believed the accused had no evil intent, they should acquit him. The jury acquitted the accused and the Lord Advocate referred the case to the High Court to determine whether the accused's evidence did amount to a defence to a charge of assault. In his opinion Lord Justice Clerk Ross stated (at p.965):

> "It has often been said that evil intention is of the essence of assault ... But what that means is that assault cannot be committed accidentally or recklessly or negligently ... In the present case, it is plain that when the accused entered the shop, presented the handgun at Mrs Daly and uttered the words which he did, he was acting deliberately. That being so, in my opinion he had the necessary intent for his actions to amount to assault, and his motive for acting as he did was irrelevant. I agree with the advocate-depute that the principle laid down by the Lord Justice-Clerk in *HM Advocate v Edmiston* would apply to the present case and that, even if the accused was believed when he stated it was a joke, his acting as he did would still constitute the crime of assault."

Lord Cowie emphasised the importance of the term evil in "evil intention". At p.968 he states in relation to the requirements for the crime of assault that "having established that the act is an evil one, all that is then required to constitute the crime of assault is that that act was done deliberately and not carelessly, recklessly or negligently". Similarly Lord Sutherland makes particular reference to both "evil" and "intention" in his opinion. At pp.969–970 he states:

> "The words 'evil intent' have an eminently respectable pedigree ... It is, however, perfectly possible to have an intention to perform particular acts without necessarily intending evil consequences from those acts. If intention means motive then plainly it is irrelevant. If, on the other hand, intention means nothing more than wilful, intentional or deliberate as opposed to accidental, careless or even reckless, then plainly it is relevant in that a criminal act cannot be performed other than deliberately ... If, therefore, a person deliberately performs an act which would in itself be criminal then both the actus reus and the mens rea coexist and a crime has been committed."

In the more recent sheriff court appeal case *S v Authority Reporter* (2012), the decision of the Sheriff Principal expresses doubt that the *Lord Advocate's Reference (No.2 of 1992)* (1992) is the leading authority on the mens rea of assault and instead suggests that it deals only with the distinction between motive and intention. It is unlikely this approach would be adopted generally, and it is more likely that the *Lord Advocate's Reference (No.2 of 1992)* will continue to be viewed as the leading authority. However, as evidenced in both *S v Authority Reporter* and also *Clark v Service* (2011) it is necessary to prove that mens rea exists. This goes beyond proving that actions by the accused were merely deliberate and instead what must be shown is that the accused's actions in relation to the victim must amount to deliberate conduct intending to cause fear, alarm or harm and thereby amount to an assault. Therefore, evil intent is still regarded as the mens rea of assault and the intention represents a deliberate action. There is no concise and agreed definition of evil, although it does still play a role in distinguishing situations where there is clearly intentional bodily harm inflicted, e.g. in the context of sport compared with that inflicted in a physical fight. Both cases involve intention. However, violence done during sport will not be regarded as criminal if it remains within the rules of the game, whereas the violence in a physical fight is capable of being "evilly intended" and, therefore, an assault.

Case law suggests that the mens rea in assault can be transferred and this is referred to as "transferred intention" (see Ch.2 for a full discussion). Where the requisite intention for assault is absent, it is open to the prosecutor to charge, e.g. causing reckless injury. This must, however, be libelled and will not be available as an alternative verdict to a charge of assault (see *HM Advocate v Harris* (1993) and the earlier section on "transferred intent" in Ch.2).

Reflex actions
As the crime of assault requires that the accused's actions are both voluntary and deliberate it has been assumed that actions that are neither of these, e.g. reflex actions, fall outwith the scope of the crime. The classification of actions as "reflex" has received little attention in reported cases with the exception of *Jessop v Johnstone* (1991). The accused, a school gym teacher, was hit on the nose with a rolled-up school jotter by a 14-year-old male pupil. He responded instantly with blows to the pupil's stomach and back. The teacher was charged with assault and at his trial the sheriff acquitted him. The prosecution appealed against this acquittal. The sheriff was of the view that the teacher had acted immediately and spontaneously and did not have the requisite mens rea of evil intent required to be convicted of assault. The prosecution appealed successfully and the High Court directed that a conviction be returned saying, inter alia, that the sheriff had confused provocation with absence of intent. Lord Justice Clerk Ross stated (at p.240):

"We appreciate that there may be cases where a person instinctively reacts to violence in a reflex way, such as if a person is suddenly and without warning struck and turns round sharply so that he comes into contact with his assailant. The present case, however, clearly did not fall within that category at all because it is plain … that the (teacher) jumped up and struck the complainer more than once … on both the stomach and back."

The court indicated that the sheriff might find that the teacher had been provoked if the evidence supported the requirements of that defence.

Attempted assault

As the actus reus of the crime of assault has been interpreted very widely, the question of an attempted assault does not arise. Remember that no harm need be inflicted for the requirement of an "attack upon the person of another" to be fulfilled. Therefore, attempts at physically hitting or alarming a person will fulfil the actus reus of assault even if the perpetrator does not carry out every aspect of the attack as intended.

Serious assault

Serious assaults are generally referred to as aggravated assaults. A number of different factors can result in an assault being aggravated. The mens rea of an aggravated assault is in many cases identical to an assault, namely evil intention. This varies, however, in some cases; for example, knowledge that the person assaulted is a police officer is necessary for the aggravated assault of "assault of a police officer" (see *Annan v Tait* (1982)). The actus reus is "an attack upon the person of another". However, characteristics of the victim or how the attack is delivered may serve to aggravate an assault.

Any feature of an assault may serve to aggravate the offence and the following are merely examples. Some of these are described as statutory aggravations, i.e. it is the provisions of a statute which dictate that the assault is aggravated in the circumstances, and others are common law aggravations.

Statutory aggravations include assault of a police officer (Police (Scotland) Act 1967 s.41) where the accused must know or reasonably believe that the person is a police officer, and racial aggravations (Crime and Disorder Act 1998 s.96) which makes it an offence either at the time of commission, or immediately before, to evince malice or ill-will towards the victim on the basis of their membership, or presumed membership, of a racial group.

Common law aggravations include the method of perpetration, e.g. where a weapon is used, "assault with a weapon"; where serious injury is caused, e.g. "assault to severe injury" or "assault to the danger of life".

Justified assault

If an assault is justified it will no longer be regarded as criminal behaviour.

Some forms of violence are justified if they occur, e.g. as part of a war, and the foundation of that justification is public policy. Three types of justification are recognised by the criminal law, namely:

(1)   justification by public policy;
(2)   justification by the victim's conduct; and
(3)   justification by the victim's consent.

(1) Justification by public policy
Certain types of violence are authorised by the state in particular contexts.

Police. The force or violence used by a police officer in securing an arrest is justified so long as it is not excessive. If it is excessive it will be treated as an assault. In *Bonar and Hogg v Macleod* (1983) the High Court held that a police officer who grasped an arrested person by the throat, twisted his arm up his back and "quick marched" him down a corridor had used excessive force in view of the fact that the prisoner was neither resisting arrest nor struggling with the officer at the time. Both the police officer and his supervising officer who witnessed this were convicted art and part of assault. In *Clark v Service* (2011), the court decided by a majority that the Crown had failed to prove that the two accused, both police officers, had the requisite mens rea of assault when they carried out arrests that were purported to be unlawful and unjustified. Lord Bonomy dissenting stated that in the absence of any reasonable grounds for Officer C forcing X (who was the complainer in respect of the incident that had brought the police to the locus, namely, an attack by a gang on his home and his car) to walk to a police vehicle and be confined against his will, his actions had properly been held to be an assault. He went on to say that when a police officer deliberately manhandled a civilian without any reasonable grounds for doing so, his conduct amounted to an attack on the victim with evil intent and therefore to assault.

Citizen's arrest. A private citizen may use reasonable force to secure a citizen's arrest where a serious crime has been committed. However, they must have witnessed the crime being committed or have equivalent information as to the identity of the perpetrator. Where the whole circumstances are so incriminating that the citizen had what amounted to a moral certainty that the accused had committed the crime, this has been recognised as equivalent to witnessing the crime being committed. In *Wightman v Lees* (2000) a citizen's arrest was effected by a person who had not actually seen the theft (of a drill) take place but had encountered the thief leaving the premises from where the drill had been stolen.

Where excessive force is used in securing such an arrest this will be treated as an assault (*Codona v Cardle* (1989)). In *Codona* the accused had not witnessed the window of his arcade being smashed but drove an employee, who had been in the arcade at the time of the incident, around the town to identify the perpetrator. When a man was pointed out to him, the arcade owner told the man he was affecting a citizen's arrest and twisted his arm behind his back. This was held to be excessive force and he was convicted of assault. The conviction was upheld on appeal as he had not witnessed the crime and had used excessive force.

The public policy reasons for restricting a citizen's right to take on the role of the police in crime detection are obvious.

Chastising children. It remains the law in Scotland that parents can physically chastise their children so long as they use moderate and reasonable force. There are cases where parents have been convicted of assault of their child because the necessary mens rea as evidenced by excessive force was used (*Peebles v McPhail* (1990)). In other cases the court has held that the loss of temper by a parent does not necessarily allow the mens rea of "evil intent" to be inferred. In *Guest v Annan* (1988) the appellant was charged with assaulting his eight-year-old daughter by repeatedly striking her on the buttocks to her injury. The father had lost his temper after his daughter lied to him about where she had been and the repeated smacking resulted in the girl bruising. He was convicted, but on appeal the High Court quashed the conviction saying that the loss of temper and displeasure with his daughter did not automatically mean that the father had the necessary mens rea of "evil intent" for the crime of assault. The power to inflict corporal punishment is now determined by s.51 of the Criminal Justice (Scotland) Act 2003. The use of excessive force by a parent may also contravene s.12(1) of the Children and Young Persons (Scotland) Act 1937, which prohibits a parent "causing or procuring the assault of their child" and art.3 of the Convention which provides that no-one shall be subjected to torture or inhuman or degrading treatment or punishment.

In each of the above cases it is clear that the courts do not only look at whether the necessary mens rea and actus reus are present but also whether the force used is reasonable. This will be decided on the circumstances of the case and, in all scenarios, if excessive force is used it is no longer justified but will be treated as an assault in its own right.

(2) Justification by the victim's conduct
If, while acting in their own or a third party's defence, an individual behaves in a way that would otherwise constitute an assault, so long as the rules of self-defence are complied with, these actions will not be regarded as an assault (*HM Advocate v Carson* (1964)). This is because the person is acting to protect himself or herself or a third party and does not have the requisite mens rea of evil intention that is required for the crime of assault. The rules of self-defence are outlined in Ch.6. It should be noted that where the rules are not met and, in particular, where any retaliation is excessive, the defending actions will be regarded as an assault (*Moore v MacDougall* (1989)).

The limited Scottish authority on the question of using force in defence of property suggests that self-defence is not available as a defence

(*McCluskey v HM Advocate* (1959)). Self-defence in respect of property was unsuccessfully pled in the English case *Martin v R.* (2001) where the accused was convicted of murder and grievous bodily harm when he shot at two retreating intruders, killing one and seriously injuring the other. At appeal this conviction was reduced to manslaughter on the ground that he was suffering from diminished responsibility. The three Appeal Court judges sentenced him to five years' imprisonment.

(3) Justification by the victim's consent

The question of whether a victim's consent to an assault would serve to elide criminal responsibility was considered in the case *Smart v HM Advocate* (1975). In *Smart* the accused was convicted of assaulting a person by kicking, punching and biting. His defence at trial was essentially that his actions could not amount to assault as the victim had accepted his invitation to a "square go", i.e. a physical fight. He also claimed that his actions were in self-defence. The sheriff had directed the jury that consent was not a defence to assault and that there was no evidence to support a plea of self-defence. The jury convicted Smart and he appealed on the grounds that consent was a defence to assault and so the sheriff had misdirected the jury.

The Appeal Court refused the appeal and in their judgment clarified the following:

(a)   Consent is not a defence to a charge of assault even where the two parties have agreed to fight. Similarly, consent is not recognised as a defence to a charge of murder (*HM Advocate v Rutherford* (1947)).

(b)   Consent is available as a defence to a charge of indecent assault because in those circumstances, where consent is present and there is no other criminal activity, the perpetrator lacks the necessary mens rea of evil intent. This can be distinguished from a physical fight where, even if there is consent to fight, the perpetrator still has the necessary evil intent when inflicting injury on their opponent.

(c)   Sporting activities which involve a degree of violence, e.g. rugby or boxing, will not be regarded as amounting to an assault where any physical injury is within the rules of the game. This is justified on the basis that the sporting competitor lacks the necessary mens rea of evil intent when acting within the rules of the game. The intention is to compete in the game rather than to inflict injury on the opponent and, therefore, the necessary mens rea for the crime of assault is missing. In distinguishing sporting activities from a "square go" the court noted (at p.66) that "where the whole purpose of the exercise is to inflict physical damage on the opponent in pursuance of a quarrel then the evil intent is present and consent is elided".

The distinction between sporting activities, e.g. boxing, and a "square go" may be difficult to sustain unless one accepts that public policy considerations may have some bearing on the distinctions drawn by the court in their judgment.

Provocation and assault

Provocation may serve to mitigate the punishment of an accused convicted of assault. While the rules of provocation are fully explored in Ch.6, an exception to the rules will be considered here. In respect of homicide only physical provocation, i.e. by real injury, is recognised. However, in respect of the crime of assault both verbal and physical provocation is recognised. Any verbal provocation requires to be inflammatory abuse which leads to an immediate loss of self-control (*Thomson v HM Advocate* (1985)). A successful plea of provocation to a charge of assault does not result in the acquittal of the accused but instead will mitigate any punishment.

RECKLESS CONDUCT

Reckless conduct crimes occur where harm or injury is inflicted on the victim, or a dangerous situation is created, and the accused lacks the mens rea of intention. Where the perpetrator has acted negligently or accidentally there will be no criminal responsibility. It is only where the actions involve a mens rea of recklessness that they will be categorised as a reckless conduct crime.

Recklessness is assessed objectively and, therefore, it is not necessary that the individual knew there was a risk and disregarded it, but instead it is enough that the reasonable person would have anticipated there was a risk.

What is recklessness?

In *Quinn v Cunningham* (1956) the court defined recklessness as "an utter disregard of what the consequences of the act in question may be so far as the public is concerned" (per Lord Justice General Clyde at p.24).

Is there a need for evidence of actual danger, damage or injury?

In *Robertson v Klos* (2006) the court held that whilst evidence of actual danger, damage or injury would make a charge easier to prove it is not always necessary. In this case, the court held that driving at 156mph on a road with a 70mph limit could not be described as anything other than culpable and reckless.

Examples of reckless conduct offences are considered below.

CRUEL AND BARBAROUS TREATMENT AND CRUEL AND UNNATURAL TREATMENT

Both of these offences involve neglect or cruel treatment of a person for whom the perpetrator is responsible. This charge was more commonly found in nineteenth-century indictments prior to children being protected by statute, including the Children and Young Persons (Scotland) Act 1937. The charge has arisen more recently in respect of the ill-treatment of a toddler who had been force fed, slapped on the legs and hands, and forced to stand unsupported and unaided for prolonged periods of time (*Bone v HM Advocate* (2005)).

CAUSING REAL INJURY

Hume (I, 327) noted that, where in an indictment terms such as assault or stabbing are not used but the conduct described nevertheless amounts to conduct which would cause real injury to a person, then that shall be treated as a criminal act no matter how new or strange the wrong. This crime, which had fallen out of use, was resurrected to deal with those instances where noxious substances, both legal and illegal, were supplied in the knowledge that they would be used in a way that was injurious to the recipient's health.

In *Khaliq v HM Advocate* (1984) the two accused were charged on indictment that they had culpably, wilfully and recklessly supplied to a number of children "glue-sniffing kits" in the knowledge of how they would be used, the dangers associated with this and that they did cause or procure the children to inhale the vapours from the solvents to the danger of their health and lives. The second charge was one of reset and related to stolen goods that had been exchanged for the "glue-sniffing kits". A preliminary plea to the relevancy of both charges was refused and leave to appeal was granted. At both the initial hearing and the appeal of the preliminary plea the court confirmed that the first charge was a crime known to the law of Scotland. The Lord Justice General (Lord Emslie) said (at p.143) referring to Hume (I, 327):

> "The general principle to be discovered from this passage is that within the category of conduct identified as criminal are acts, whatever their nature may be, which cause real injury to the person. Does this case, though never before occurring on its facts, fall within that general principle … ? In my opinion it does."

The opinion of the court also states that the consent of the victim, in their action of inhaling the substance, does not elide the criminal responsibility of the accused. The age of the children was not held to be essential to the relevancy of the charge, but would be relevant in determining whether the supply complained of ought to be held to have been a cause of the injury suffered. The court also considered whether there was a causal link between the actions of the accused and the harm suffered. This is discussed in more detail in Ch.2.

The requisite actus reus and mens rea of this crime is not clear in *Khaliq*, although the direction to the jury in *Ulhaq v HM Advocate* (1990) defines what is required in the context of supply of noxious substances. The accused in *Ulhaq* was charged with essentially the same crime as had arisen in *Khaliq*. The charge was one of "culpably and recklessly endangering the lives and health of a number of people in their twenties by selling them a substantial quantity of various solvents, knowing that the recipients intended to use them for inhaling their vapours and that such inhalation would be injurious to their health, and to the danger of their lives, and with causing or procuring said inhalation to the danger of the recipients' health and lives." (p.593)

The jury were directed that the crime charged required proof that there was the culpable, wilful and reckless supply of certain items for the purpose of abuse, and that these were supplied in the knowledge of how they were to be used and that this would be injurious to health and to the danger of the recipients' lives.

Presumably, the actus reus of this crime could be fulfilled by a variety of means including supply and administration. There is no requirement for "an attack" which is necessary for the crime of assault. While this is a crime of recklessness, the direction to the jury in *Ulhaq* focuses on the knowledge of the accused both of the purpose for which the substances are to be used and the effect of their use. It is this requirement of knowledge that distinguishes this crime from reckless injury.

RECKLESS INJURY

This crime involves unintentionally but recklessly causing injury to another. In *HM Advocate v Harris* (1993) the accused, a night-club bouncer, was charged with assaulting a woman to her severe injury and permanent disfigurement by seizing hold of her, pushing her on the body and causing her to fall down a flight of stairs and onto a roadway as a result of which she was struck by a passing motor vehicle. There was an alternative charge of culpably, wilfully and recklessly seizing hold of the woman, pushing her on the body and causing her to fall down a flight of stairs and onto the roadway as a result of which she was struck by a motor vehicle to her severe injury and permanent disfigurement. An objection to the relevancy of the alternative charge was sustained by the sheriff and thereafter successfully appealed by the Crown to the High Court. A bench of five judges held that a charge of reckless conduct did not require to be libelled as being "to the danger of the lieges" before it was relevant and thereby partially overruled the decision in *Quinn v Cunningham* (1956). The court also rejected the submission that both charges libelled the same crime and were therefore not truly alternatives. The court held, by majority, with Lord McCluskey dissenting, that, although the same conduct was libelled in both charges, they were distinguished by the mens rea required for each crime, i.e. assault requires intent whereas reckless conduct/injury requires a mens rea of recklessness. Lord McCluskey dissenting said (at p.969K–L):

"[W]here one has got an averment of wilful seizing of a person and pushing her on the body thereby causing her to fall down a flight of stairs there is absolutely no need to invent an innominate crime. The familiar crime of assault fits the bill perfectly ... In my opinion, the alternative charge in the indictment is irrelevant on the ground that it does not disclose a crime known to the law of Scotland. In my opinion, there is no crime known to the law of Scotland consisting of wilfully seizing another human being, pushing her on the body and causing her to fall down a flight of stairs, except the crime of assault. As *ex hypothesi* the alternative charge does not contain a charge of assault it cannot be relevant."

RECKLESSLY ENDANGERING THE LIEGES

This crime is distinguishable from reckless injury in that it will be charged where an accused has created a dangerous situation that may have placed the public in danger, even though no actual injury has been caused. The dangerous situation can be the result of the reckless performing of either a lawful or an unlawful act. Many cases in this category involve the reckless discharge of firearms, e.g. in *Cameron v Maguire* (1999) the offence is libelled as "you did recklessly discharge a loaded rifle in the direction of open woodland to the danger of the lieges who might reasonably be expected to be walking there". However, other types of behaviour have been libelled as recklessly endangering the lieges, e.g. "culpably and recklessly promoting and organising a rave in a derelict warehouse to the danger of the lieges" in *Normand v Robinson* (1994).

ILL-TREATMENT OF CHILDREN

Section 12 of the Children and Young Persons (Scotland) Act 1937 makes it an offence to wilfully assault, neglect, ill-treat or abandon a child or to expose him or cause or procure for these things to happen. *McF v Normand* (1995) and other cases prosecuted under s.12 relate to the wilful neglect of children and often involve children being left unattended. In this case an 18-month-old was left in a car on a busy street while the parents went shopping. The sheriff convicted on account of the fact that the child had been exposed to various risks, e.g. sudden illness, kidnap, car theft, although nothing actually happened and there was no evidence that the child was distressed or harmed. The High Court held on appeal that the matters relied upon by the sheriff were speculative and not related to any particular period the child was alone in the car. The court held that the sheriff was not entitled to take the decision he did on the evidence presented.

HOMICIDE

Two types of criminal homicide are recognised in Scots law: murder and culpable homicide. Not all deaths result in a charge of murder or culpable homicide. Where the actions of the accused are negligent or accidental this will not result in a charge of murder nor culpable homicide as the accused lacks the necessary mens rea. As noted in Ch.2, negligence is not a recognised form of mens rea. Accidental or negligent homicide is often referred to as casual homicide. Alison defined casual homicide as

> "where a person kills unintentionally, when lawfully employed, and neither meaning harm to anyone, nor having failed in the due degree of care and circumspection for preventing mischief to his neighbour." (*Criminal Law*, Vol. I, pp.139–140)

An example is given of where a person's gun discharges in his hand and kills his neighbour.

Where the killing of another person is deemed to be justified, the law will treat such actions as non-criminal homicides. Homicide can be justified by a number of factors including death caused by the armed forces in the context of war, or where a person acting in self-defence kills an attacker. The requirements of self-defence are examined in Ch.6.

Actus reus
The actus reus of both murder and culpable homicide is the destruction of human life other than one's own. There is no time-limit within which death must result. However, there must be a causal connection between the actions of the accused and the harm suffered. As there is no time limit, an accused who has been convicted of assaulting his victim may also be prosecuted at a later date for murder or culpable homicide should the victim subsequently die from the injuries inflicted. The principle of res judicata will not apply to such a scenario and prevent the additional prosecution for the new crime.

Destruction of life
It is necessary for a charge of homicide that life is actually destroyed. Although there is not a legal definition of death, it is assumed to involve the permanent cessation of all brain activity. For life to have been destroyed it is necessary that the victim of homicide had been alive. This means that a child must be born and have a separate existence of its own before it is regarded as a living human being. Where death is caused by injures received in the womb, so long as the baby has lived for a short time outside the womb, it will be relevant to charge murder or culpable homicide in respect of the injuries. If the baby does not survive outside the womb, then the perpetrator could only be charged with a crime related to injuring the pregnant woman. In *McCluskey v HM Advocate* (1989) the accused was charged with causing death by reckless driving. The victim, a baby, had

been *in utero* at the time of the accident but had lived a short time outside the womb before death.

Suicide
A further requirement is that the life taken must be other than one's own. Although suicide and attempted suicide are not crimes in Scotland, where one person kills another as part of a "suicide pact" and then survives, they have fulfilled the legal requirements for the crime of murder, but in practice will be charged with culpable homicide.

Differences between murder and culpable homicide
As noted above, the actus reus of murder and culpable homicide is identical. The crimes are distinguished by the punishment each attracts and the mens rea. In all common law crimes, except murder, the punishment is at the discretion of the sentencer within the statutory limits that are laid down. In the case of murder, the punishment is a mandatory life sentence, whereas for culpable homicide, the sentence is at the discretion of the judge. The mens rea of each crime differ and are explored below. It should be noted that it is competent to return a verdict of culpable homicide to a charge of murder on the basis that the mens rea of culpable homicide rather than murder can be inferred from the evidence. For this reason, judges should direct juries that an alternative verdict of culpable homicide is available unless they are satisfied that there is no basis at all for the verdict in the evidence (*Ferguson v HM Advocate* (2009)).

Mens rea of murder
The classic definition of the crime of murder is given by Macdonald as:

> "[M]urder is constituted by a wilful act causing the destruction of life, whether intended to kill, or displaying such wicked recklessness as to imply a disposition depraved enough to be regardless of the consequences." (*A Practical Treatise on the Criminal Law of Scotland*, 5th edn (1948), p.89.)

It is generally accepted that there are two mens reae for the crime of murder. These are (wicked) intention and wicked recklessness. As in all other crimes, the mens rea of the accused will be inferred from the circumstances. Therefore, although murder is a result crime, i.e. we are interested in the result of the actions of the accused and not the conduct, the conduct will give us an insight into the mens rea of the accused.

Wicked intention
The mens rea of any crime is the mental state of the accused at the time the crime was committed. As a consequence, motive and premeditation are not relevant. Intention is, therefore, judged at the time the act was committed. Macdonald and the majority of case law refer to the mens rea of murder as "intention". While this continued to be viewed as a correct statement of the

law, in *Drury v HM Advocate* (2001) a bench of five judges held that the mens rea of murder was wicked recklessness or "wicked intention to kill", which departs from both Macdonald's definition and the mere "intention to kill" which has been referred to in other cases. In *Drury*, Lord Justice General Rodger observed at p.589, that "saying that the perpetrator 'wickedly' intends to kill is just a shorthand way of referring to what Hume (vol I p.254) describes the 'murderer's wicked and mischievous purpose' in contradistinction to 'those motives of necessity, duty or allowable infirmity, which may serve to justify or excuse' the deliberate taking of life".

In *Elsherkisi v HM Advocate* (2011) the court confirmed that, where there is an absence of justification or mitigation (i.e. the accused had not pled self-defence, provocation or diminished responsibility), it would be sufficient for the trial judge to direct the jury that, if they concluded that the accused intentionally killed his victim, they should convict him of murder. Jury directions as to "wicked intention to kill" as opposed to "intention to kill" will only arise in those cases where the accused has pled self-defence, provocation or diminished responsibility. This is because it is the absence of self-defence, provocation or diminished responsibility which is deemed to make the accused's intention a "wicked" intention. If no such defence is pled then the jury will be directed that the mens rea of murder is intention to kill or wicked recklessness, as suggested by Macdonald (*Arthur v HM Advocate* (2002)).

Consent, intention and murder

The general rule in criminal law that a person cannot consent to harm being done to them is followed in respect of both murder and culpable homicide. In *HM Advocate v Rutherford* (1947) the accused was charged with murder of a woman. He gave evidence that the woman had requested that he strangle her with his tie and that she had put the tie around her neck. He told the court that he had pulled the tie and, on the woman telling him to get on with it, he had pulled it again. He said that he had not intended to harm the woman but only to frighten or humour her. When he discovered she was dead he had reported the matter to the police. Under cross-examination he admitted that he must have used a strong pull of the necktie and that he was aware that such actions involved a good chance of choking the victim to death. Medical evidence referred to the presence of both tie marks and hand marks on the woman's neck with the latter being consistent with manual strangling. Lord Justice Clerk Cooper directed the jury to reject the defence submission that the actions of the accused amounted to casual homicide. On the question of the consent of the victim he said (at pp.5–6):

> "[I]f life is taken under circumstances which would otherwise infer guilt of murder, the crime does not cease to be murder merely because the victim consented to be murdered, or even urged the assailant to strike the fatal blow … The attitude of the victim is irrelevant. What matters is the intent of the assailant."

In *Sutherland v HM Advocate* (1994) the victim was party to a common plan, the execution of which resulted in his death. The court held that the victim's consent could not turn a criminal act into one which was not criminal. In *Scott v HM Advocate* (2012), the court observed that there may be a distinction to be drawn between cases such as *Rutherford*, where the conduct involved was such that consent would not impact on whether the mens rea test for murder was met, and other cases, where in the objective assessment of whether wicked recklessness had been demonstrated by the behaviour of the accused, the likely impact of consent upon that conduct might have a role to play. In *Scott*, the accused had been convicted of assault and murder of X. S and X had spent the day consuming alcohol before joining H and D who along with S were heroin users. S and H injected themselves with heroin and H assisted D to do so. H informed S that X was not a heroin user and stated that the mixture prepared by S for administration to X was too strong. Although S indicated he would only inject X with some of the mixture he injected the total amount into X's arm.

The consent of the victim has similarly not reduced the responsibility of a person who kills to relieve the victim from suffering or who survives a suicide pact having killed the other party. In both instances the perpetrator has demonstrated the necessary intention to kill required for the crime of murder although in practice this is prosecuted as culpable homicide (*HM Advocate v Brady* (1997)).

Intention to do serious bodily harm

Reference to the existence of a second form of intentional mens rea for the crime of murder, namely "intention to do serious bodily harm", has been referred to in some cases including *HM Advocate v Hartley* (1989) and *HM Advocate v Cawthorne* (1968). This is now largely accepted as being an error. Note, however, that the seriousness of injuries inflicted may assist in drawing an inference of an intention to kill.

Wicked recklessness

The case of *Cawthorne v HM Advocate* (1968) confirmed wicked recklessness as a separate mens rea for the crime of murder. Wicked recklessness can be inferred in cases where the accused does not have a deliberate intention to kill but acts with such wicked recklessness as to show that they are indifferent as to whether or not death results. Thus, wicked recklessness requires something more than mere recklessness, which has been defined as "a total indifference to and disregard for the safety of the public" (*RHW v HM Advocate* (1982) at p.420). Hume suggests that there are three requirements for this form of mens rea:

(1)   the accused should have meant to perpetrate some great and outrageous bodily harm;

(2)   the harm was such as might well have resulted in death; and

(3)   the harm showed an absolute or utter indifference as to whether the victim lived or died (B.R. Bell, *Commentaries on the Law of*

Scotland Respecting Crimes, 4th edn (reprinted 1986), Vol. I, pp.191, 238 and 256).

Gordon (para.23.33) states that "there is murder wherever death is caused with wicked intention to kill or by an act intended to cause physical injury and displaying a wicked disregard of fatal consequences". This definition was confirmed in *HM Advocate v Purcell* (2007), where the court held that, for the crime of murder, it was essential that the Crown libelled a wilful act intended to cause physical injury. In the more recent five bench decision in *Petto v HM Advocate* (2012), the accused had set fire to a tenement building for the purpose of destroying a dead body contained therein. A resident of the tenement, unconnected with the accused, died as a result of the fire. The court held that where a person starts a major fire on the ground floor of such a building the inevitable conclusion is that it must be done in the certain knowledge that those in the building would be at risk of death or serious injury, and the acceptance of that risk must be equated with an intention that the consequences should occur.

It is sometimes, incorrectly, assumed that the use of weapons in the perpetration of any crime where death occurs will result in a charge of murder. This assumption may be partly attributable to the direction to the jury by Lord Justice Clerk Aitchison in *HM Advocate v McGuinness* (1937) (p.40) that

> "people who use knives and pokers and hatchets against a fellow citizen are not entitled to say 'we did not mean to kill', if death results. If people resort to the use of deadly weapons of this kind, they are guilty of murder, whether or not they intended to kill."

This is not wholly accurate, as the use of these weapons allow an inference to be drawn that the accused meant to perpetrate some great and outrageous bodily harm, that the harm was such as might well have resulted in death and that the harm showed an absolute or utter indifference as to whether the victim lived or died, i.e. the requirements of wicked recklessness. The question in these circumstances is whether the mens rea for murder can be inferred from all of the circumstances, including the use of weapons. The more lethal or dangerous the weapons used the easier it will be to infer the mens rea of murder (*Broadley v HM Advocate* (1991)). The actions of the accused after an incident can be taken into account when inferring their mens rea (*Halliday v HM Advocate* (1998)).

Mens rea of culpable homicide
The mens rea of culpable homicide is recklessness. As noted above recklessness has been defined as "a total indifference to and disregard for the safety of the public" (*RHW v HM Advocate* (1982) at p.420). Macdonald described culpable homicide as where death is caused by improper conduct but the guilt is less than murder. Where an accused is charged with murder and successfully pleads a mitigating defence, e.g.

provocation, they will be convicted of culpable homicide. The crime of culpable homicide applies to non-intentional killing where the mens rea is recklessness and intentional killing where a mitigating defence is available to the accused.

Hume deals with four categories of culpable homicide:

(1)   An assault that results in death where there is no inference of intention or wicked recklessness.
(2)   Death that results in the course of another unlawful act where the mens rea is recklessness.
(3)   Where death occurs in the performance of a lawful act.
(4)   Where the accused has the requisite mens rea for the crime of murder but a mitigating defence, e.g. provocation or diminished responsibility, serve to mitigate the responsibility of the accused (I, 233–247).

Hume's four categories will be examined under the headings "voluntary" and "involuntary" culpable homicide. While the terms "voluntary", "involuntary" and Hume's four classifications are useful tools which we employ to examine culpable homicide, it should be remembered that there is only one crime of culpable homicide. It is, therefore, not correct to refer to a criminal charge of voluntary culpable homicide or involuntary culpable homicide. In both of these instances the crime is culpable homicide.

Involuntary culpable homicide
This category of culpable homicide arises where death is caused unintentionally without the requisite degree of wicked recklessness or intention required for murder. It may take place in the course of a lawful or unlawful act and the mens rea is recklessness. This category of culpable homicide will be examined using three of Hume's (four) categories referred to above.

(1) An assault that results in death. Where death results either in the course of an assault or as a result of an assault this will be charged at least as culpable homicide. The decision on whether the charge should be murder or culpable homicide is determined by the mens rea. The level of violence used in an assault will be very important in determining the mens rea and, where severe violence has been used, there is more chance that the mens rea of murder, intention or wicked recklessness, will be inferred. Where death results from a minor assault and only recklessness can be inferred, culpable homicide will be charged. In *Bird v HM Advocate* (1952) the accused followed a woman whom he believed had taken his money. When the victim tried to get into a car the accused pulled her out. Her weak heart and the threatening nature of the situation combined to cause her death. Bird was charged with culpable homicide. During the trial it was accepted that the accused would not have contemplated any risk of serious harm to his victim. In his charge to the jury the judge made it clear that the wrongful conduct required for a culpable homicide conviction could include no more than a mere threatening gesture. The jury returned a verdict of guilty.

(2) Death that results in the course of another unlawful act. Where death occurs in the course of a crime other than assault this may also be charged as culpable homicide. The Crown will require to prove that the accused acted with a mens rea of recklessness. Once again, where there is evidence of wicked intent or wicked recklessness a charge of murder would be appropriate. Culpable homicide will be charged where death results from a criminal act, the nature of which, or the degree of recklessness employed is such, that the risk of personal injury was reasonably forseeable. Not every criminal act which results in death will fulfil this requirement. Fire-raising to defraud insurers was not viewed as fulfilling this requirement by the trial judge in *Sutherland v HM Advocate* (1994). The trial judge directed the jury that it is not unlawful to set fire to your own house and, as an intention to defraud insurers is not an offence against the person, it does not convert a lawful act of setting fire to one's own house into an unlawful act for the purposes of the law relating to culpable homicide. Therefore, it was necessary for the Crown to prove that the fire-raising was done by the accused in the face of obvious risks which were foreseeable or done in circumstances which showed a complete disregard for any potential dangers which might result. The question for the jury was, consequently, had the accused acted recklessly and did his actions cause the death of the victim with whom he had been acting in concert?

Unlawful acts resulting in death which have resulted in a conviction of culpable homicide include where death resulted from reckless fire-raising (*Mathieson v HM Advocate* (1981)) and the unreported case of *Finnigan* (1958) (see Gordon, *Criminal Law*, para.26.27) where death of an occupant of a building was the consequence of the accused stealing a gas meter by wrenching it from its supply pipe. In *Lord Advocate's Reference (No.1 of 1994)* (1995) it was held that a conviction of culpable homicide could result from the supply of a controlled drug to a recipient who died following ingestion. (The causation issues which arise in the last case are similar to those addressed by the court in *Khaliq v HM Advocate* (1984), see Ch.2.) *MacAngus* (2009) confirms that the Crown must prove that any supply was reckless.

(3) Where death occurs in the performance of a lawful act. A charge of culpable homicide arising from a recklessly performed lawful act requires recklessness and not merely carelessness or negligence on the part of the accused. Reported cases include road traffic offences, e.g. *Paton v HM Advocate* (1935). However, similar cases now tend to be prosecuted under s.1 of the Road Traffic Act 1988, "causing death by dangerous driving". The reckless navigation of a boat (*Angus MacPherson and John Stewart* (1861)) and the reckless installation of a gas fire, where the failure to provide flues resulted in the death of two people from carbon monoxide poisoning (*Ross Fontana* (1990) Unreported, see Jones and Christie, p.255), both resulted in charges of culpable homicide.

Voluntary culpable homicide
The term voluntary culpable homicide is used to describe those situations where the accused is deemed to have killed intentionally or with wicked recklessness, i.e. have fulfilled the requirements for the crime of murder, but due to mitigating circumstances they are deemed to be guilty of culpable homicide. In these circumstances, the accused must have acted under provocation or diminished responsibility before their actions will be classified as the crime of culpable homicide. The requirements of provocation and diminished responsibility are considered in Ch.6.

As a matter of policy, certain types of conduct, which in law amount to murder, are charged as culpable homicide. These include suicide pacts where one of the parties survive, and assisted euthanasia (*HM Advocate v Brady* (1997)).

Attempted murder and culpable homicide
The crime of attempted murder will be charged where the actions of the accused are such that death could have occurred and the accused has displayed the criminal intention or wicked recklessness found in the crime of murder (*Cawthorne v HM Advocate* (1968)). The implicit recognition of a reckless attempt in the decision in *Cawthorne* departs from the traditional approach wherein reckless attempts were not recognised. The traditional approach continues to be followed in respect of attempted culpable homicide and there is no record of such a crime ever having been charged. The absence of a crime of attempted culpable homicide means that, where conduct amounts to the crime of attempted murder but either provocation or diminished responsibility mitigates the responsibility of the accused, the appropriate verdict is one of assault (*Salmond v HM Advocate* (1991); *HM Advocate v Blake* (1986)).

EXTORTION

The actus reus of extortion is a threat accompanied by a demand and the mens rea is intention. There must be an actual threat, either express or implied, and where this is absent a demand on its own is not enough (*HM Advocate v Donoghue* (1971)). The demand will generally be for money but it is not restricted to this. In *Rae v Donnelly* (1982) the accused threatened to disclose alleged sexual impropriety unless the demand for resignation by one of the parties and the abandonment of a claim of unfair dismissal by the other was met. The crime of extortion requires that the demand be met. Where the demand is not met the accused may be convicted of attempted extortion (*Black v Carmichael*; *Carmichael v Black* (1992)). In *Black v Carmichael*; *Carmichael v Black* Lord Justice General Hope stated (at p.717):

"In my opinion, it is extortion to seek to enforce a legitimate debt by means which the law regards as illegitimate, just as it is extortion to seek by such means to obtain money or some other advantage to which the accused has no right at all."

SEXUAL OFFENCES AGAINST THE PERSON

The main common law sexual offences have been codified by the Sexual Offences (Scotland) Act 2009 which came into force on December 1, 2010. This Act redefines the crime of rape and creates some new offences. The Act categorises offences according to the complainer. There are three broad categories of complainer: adults, older children (13–16 years) and young children (under 13 years). The main offences contained within the Act criminalise rape, sexual assault by penetration, sexual assault, sexual coercion, coercing another to be present during sexual activity, coercing a person to look at a sexual image, communicating indecently, sexual exposure, voyeurism and administering a substance for sexual purposes. Some of the new offences reflect the use of modern technology in perpetuating sexual offences, e.g. the offence of voyeurism is to be extended by the Criminal Justice and Licensing Act 2010 to include covertly taking images of underwear or genitals. The three main offences for the purposes of this text are rape, sexual assault by penetration and sexual assault.

It should be noted that the previous common law provisions in this area are yet to be repealed. Therefore, there is the unusual situation where both statutory and common law provisions relating to effectively the same subject matter are in force simultaneously. This section will focus only on the statutory provisions; however, details of the common law provisions can be found in the 2nd Edition of this text.

Rape
Section 1 of the 2009 Act provides:
(1)   If a person ("A"), with A's penis—
      (a)   without another person ("B") consenting, and
      (b)   without any reasonable belief that B consents,
      penetrates to any extent, either intending to do so or reckless as to whether there is penetration, the vagina, anus or mouth of B then A commits an offence, to be known as the offence of rape.
(2)   For the purposes of this section, penetration is a continuing act from entry until withdrawal of the penis; but this subsection is subject to subsection (3).
(3)   In a case where penetration is initially consented to but at some point of time the consent is withdrawn, subsection (2) is to be construed as if the reference in it to a continuing act from entry were a reference to a continuing act from that point of time.

(4)   In this Act—
"penis" includes a surgically constructed penis if it forms part of A, having been created in the course of surgical treatment, and "vagina" includes—
(a)   the vulva, and
(b)   a surgically constructed vagina (together with any surgically constructed vulva), if it forms part of B, having been created in the course of such treatment.

Rape is defined in s.1 of the Act to involve penetration to any extent of the vagina, anus or mouth with a penis. Whilst the perpetrator of this crime remains male, the new provisions include men within the category of victims of rape. The actus reus of the crime is penetration by the perpetrator's penis of the complainer's vagina, anus or mouth. Penetration is a continuing act and the provisions allow for a person who has initially consented to penetration to withdraw that consent. The mens rea of the crime of rape is intention or recklessness. The Crown require to prove that the complainer did not consent to the act of penetration and that the perpetrator either intended to act without the complainer's consent or was reckless as to whether or not they consented. The Crown will also require to prove an absence of reasonable belief that there was consent.

Consent
The provisions around consent apply to all of the offences set out in Part 1 of the Act (applying to adults). Consent is defined as "free agreement" in s.12. A mentally disordered person is incapable of consenting to conduct set out in ss.1–9. Consent is assessed at the time the conduct takes place and there are a number of situations, set out in s.13, where it is assumed that free agreement to conduct is absent including when the complainer is incapable of giving consent to conduct because of the effect of alcohol or any other substance; threats of violence; unlawful detainment; deception as to the nature or purpose of the conduct; impersonating a person personally known to the complainer or where indication of agreement is given by someone other than the complainer. The effect of any of the above conditions is to negate consent previously given. Although consent is assumed to be absent in the foregoing scenarios, it has been suggested by A.N. Brown (at p.8).

> "that unless the accused is to be deemed to know that the *tempus inspiciendum* (time for assessing) for consent is the time when the sexual act takes place and that earlier expressions of consent are ineffective, proof of that earlier indication of general consent—perhaps even by a concession by the complainer in cross examination—will be a foundation for an argument that reasonable belief is not excluded".

It is an offence to administer alcohol or drugs to the complainer, or cause the complainer to take a substance, without their knowledge or any reasonable belief that the complainer knows, in order to stupefy the complainer so as to enable any person to engage in sexual activity. Section 14 provides that a person is incapable of consent whilst asleep or unconscious, but it does not provide that falling asleep or losing consciousness constitutes a withdrawal of consent previously given.

The question of ability to consent to penile penetration where all parties to the conduct are older children is dealt with in s.37. This section makes it an offence for children aged between 13 and 16 years to engage consensually in penile penetration of the vagina, anus or mouth or in oral sex. It will be necessary for the Crown to prove that both parties consented before such activity will be prosecuted under this section. Where the perpetrator of penile penetration has reached 16 years of age, but the others are older children, i.e. aged 13 to 16 years, s.28 creates an offence of having intercourse with an older child. The actus reus of this offence is the penetration of the vagina, anus or mouth with the perpetrator's penis. The Crown do not require to prove either absence of consent or absence of a reasonable belief that there was consent. A defence to all of the "older children" offences is available in s.39. It is a defence where the perpetrator had a reasonable belief that the complainer had attained the age of 16, provided that he has not previously been charged by the police with a sexual offence, and he is not subject to a sexual harm order. Children below the age of 13 are not deemed capable of consenting to any sexual activity.

Sexual assault by penetration
Section 2 of the 2009 Act provides:
(1)   If a person ("A"), with any part of A's body or anything else—
        (a)   without another person ("B") consenting, and
        (b)   without any reasonable belief that B consents,
        penetrates sexually to any extent, either intending to do so or
        reckless as to whether there is penetration, the vagina or anus of B
        then A commits an offence, to be known as the offence of sexual
        assault by penetration.
(2)   For the purposes of this section, penetration is a continuing act
        from entry to withdrawal of whatever is intruded; but this
        subsection is subject to subsection (3).
(3)   In a case where penetration is initially consented to but at some
        point of time the consent is withdrawn, subsection (2) is to be
        construed as if the reference in it to a continuing act from entry were
        a reference to a continuing act from that point of time.
(4)   Without prejudice to the generality of subsection (1), the reference
        in that subsection to penetration with any part of A's body is to be
        construed as including a reference to penetration with A's penis.

This section provides that a person is guilty of an offence if, without consent or any reasonable belief that there is consent, they penetrate sexually with any means and to any extent, either intending to do so or recklessly, the complainer's vagina or anus. This section includes penile penetration (as does s.1) as well as penetration with other objects. The perpetrator and victim of this offence could be male or female except where penetration involves the perpetrator's penis which can only be carried out by a man.

Sexual assault

Section 3 of the 2009 Act provides:

(1)   If a person ("A")—

    (a)   without another person ("B") consenting, and

    (b)   without any reasonable belief that B consents,

    does any of the things mentioned in subsection (2), then A commits an offence, to be known as the offence of sexual assault.

(2)   Those things are, that A—

    (a)   penetrates sexually, by any means and to any extent, either intending to do so or reckless as to whether there is penetration, the vagina, anus or mouth of B,

    (b)   intentionally or recklessly touches B sexually,

    (c)   engages in any other form of sexual activity in which A, intentionally or recklessly, has physical contact (whether bodily contact or contact by means of an implement and whether or not through clothing) with B,

    (d)   intentionally or recklessly ejaculates semen onto B,

    (e)   intentionally or recklessly emits urine or saliva onto B sexually.

(3)   For the purposes of paragraph (a) of subsection (2), penetration is a continuing act from entry until withdrawal of whatever is intruded; but this subsection is subject to subsection (4).

(4)   In a case where penetration is initially consented to but at some point of time the consent is withdrawn, subsection (3) is to be construed as if the reference in it to a continuing act from entry were a reference to a continuing act from that point of time.

(5)   Without prejudice to the generality of paragraph (a) of subsection (2), the reference in the paragraph to penetration by any means is to be construed as including a reference to penetration with A's penis.

This section outlines the offence of sexual assault with ss.20 and 30 respectively dealing with the sexual assault of young and older children. The mens rea of sexual assault is intention or recklessness. The Act states that if A without another person consenting or, without any reasonable belief that they consent does any of the things mentioned in subsection (2), then A commits an offence to be known as sexual assault. The activities deemed to fall within the ambit of sexual assault include: penetration sexually of the vagina, anus or mouth, by any means and to any extent; intentionally or recklessly touching sexually; engaging in any form of sexual activity which involves physical contact either directly using bodily parts or indirectly using implements either onto skin or clothing; intentionally or recklessly ejaculating semen, and intentionally or recklessly emitting urine or saliva onto B sexually. As with rape, penetration is deemed to be a continuing act and consent can be withdrawn at any time. There is clearly an overlap with ss.1 and 2, as s.3 also refers to penetration with A's penis. Except in the case of penile penetration, the perpetrator can be male or female. This offence can be committed against males or females.

READING

T. Jones and M. Christie, *Criminal Law*, 5th edn (Edinburgh: W. Green & Son, 2012), Ch.9.

C. Gane, C. Stoddart and J. Chalmers, *A Casebook on Scottish Criminal Law*, 4th edn (Edinburgh, W. Green & Son, 2009), Chs 8–10.

G.H. Gordon, *Criminal Law*, M. Christie, ed., 3rd edn (Edinburgh: W. Green & Son, 2000), Vol. II.

A.N. Brown, *Sexual Offences (Scotland) Act 2009* (Edinburgh: W. Green & Son, 2009).

4. CRIMES OF DISHONESTY
AND AGAINST PROPERTY

THEFT

The definition of the crime of theft has changed over time. The definition given by Hume was "the felonious taking and carrying away of the property of another, for profit". The crime was strictly defined and required the actual taking of property, the intention to permanently deprive the owner and that the taking must be for profit. This strict definition was due to theft being a capital offence at that time. The modern definition of theft can be described as having an actus reus of appropriation, which incorporates theft achieved by taking or finding, and a mens rea of intention, although it is no longer restricted to an intention permanently to deprive the owner of their property. The requirement "for lucre", i.e. profit, no longer applies to theft and it is the owner's loss rather than the other's gain which is important (*Black v Carmichael; Carmichael v Black* (1992)). The current definition of theft can be stated as:

> *The taking or appropriation of the goods or property of another without the consent of the owner and with the intent to deprive them of that property.*

The modern law of theft continues to develop with questions over what can be stolen, e.g. computer data; how something can be stolen, e.g. depriving the owner of the use of their property; and what form an intention to deprive should take, e.g. permanent, indefinite, or temporary. The current definition of theft can be broken into the following elements:

(1)   the appropriation;
(2)   of the property of another which is capable of being stolen;
(3)   without the consent of the owner; and
(4)   with the intention to deprive the owner of that property.

The first three of these requirements relate to the actus reus and the fourth to the mens rea.

Actus reus of theft
(1)Taking or appropriation
Appropriation is now assumed to cover theft by taking, theft by finding and also where goods already in possession are appropriated. Hume's definition of theft did not include those circumstances where a person found goods and retained them or where a person who is in possession of goods, with the consent of the owner, appropriates them for his own use. Appropriation includes: where goods are taken from the owner without

their consent (*Barr v O'Brien* (1991)); where goods given for one purpose are used for another (*Dewar v HM Advocate* (1945)); where the owner is prevented from using his goods (*Black v Carmichael*; *Carmichael v Black* (1992)); and where goods found are appropriated for the finder's own use (*John Smith* (1838); *MacMillan v Lowe* (1991)).

In addition to the common law provisions which recognise theft by finding, there are statutory provisions. The Civic Government (Scotland) Act 1982 ss.67 to 75 provide that it is an offence if the finder of property fails to take reasonable care of it and report the finding to the police or the owner/occupier of the premises where the property was found. If a person finding property contravenes this provision they will not only have breached the statute but their actions will allow the mens rea of theft, namely intention, to be inferred from their actions.

Where theft is of goods already in the possession of the thief, the crime is committed at the point the custodier forms the intention to deprive the owner of their goods by appropriating them. Evidence of this intention is, of course, necessary and may be more difficult to infer than in the case of theft by taking. As a result, it is almost impossible in such cases to differentiate the actus reus and mens rea of theft. There is no act of taking and the thief is authorised to possess and, in some cases, to carry out certain acts involving the property. Therefore, the conduct of the accused must be examined to infer at which point the intention to appropriate the goods was formed.

In *Dewar* the accused, a manager of a crematorium, was convicted of the theft of two coffins and the lids of a large number of other coffins. In a statement to the police Dewar admitted the practice of retaining the coffins and said that this was the general practice throughout the crematorium movement. The appropriation of the property was fulfilled at the point Dewar retained the coffins and lids rather than incinerating them. In *Carmichael* the accused was charged with the crime of extortion and, alternatively, the theft of two cars. The accused had wheel clamped the cars and placed a notice on the windscreen stating that the clamp would be removed upon payment of a fine. The cars were parked in a private car park without permission. In this case, the property was appropriated at the point the wheel was clamped, thereby depriving the owners of the use of their property.

Dewar may suggest that appropriation requires that the accused has assumed the full rights of the owner in respect of the appropriated property. However, *Carmichael* illustrates that it is not necessary for either the owner of the goods to have given over their full rights in the property or for the accused to have assumed the full rights of the owner.

Theft by appropriation is fully explained in *Black v Carmichael*; *Carmichael v Black* (1992) (at pp.719–720), where the Lord Justice General Hope said:

> "[T]he essential feature of the physical act necessary to constitute theft is the appropriation, by which control and possession of the thing

is taken from its owner or custodier. In principle, therefore, the removal of the thing does not seem to be necessary, if the effect of the act which is done to it is its appropriation by the accused ... It seems to me that the act of depriving the motorist of the use of his motor-car by detaining it against his will can accurately be described as stealing something from him and that, on this basis, the facts libelled are sufficient to constitute a charge of theft. The accused are said to have deliberately placed a wheel clamp on a wheel of a vehicle which they found in the car park, in order to detain it there and keep it under their control against the will of the motorist. There is no suggestion that it was intended by the motorist that they (the accused) should have control over the car for any purpose, or that by parking the vehicle in the car park he (the motorist) intended that anyone else should have control over it. And the physical element of appropriation is clearly present, in my opinion, since the purpose and effect of the wheel clamp was to immobilise the vehicle and to deprive the motorist of his possession and use of it as [a] motor car."

(2) Property of another capable of being stolen

Before property can be stolen it requires to be publicly or privately owned by another person, capable of being moved and must be corporeal. In general, people cannot steal their own property. The possible exception to this would be that the directors of a company could be held liable for stealing from the company (*Sandlan v HM Advocate* (1983)). Remember, however, that the company is a separate legal entity so it is not the same as stealing your own property.

Moveable corporeal property. Generally, the rule is that something must be moveable (corporeal property) before it can be stolen. Consequently, land cannot be stolen but things that are grown on the land may be stolen. Money and documents which contain the person's right to a thing, e.g. share certificates, can be stolen. On the basis of taking the document that represents the incorporeal property, e.g. the share certificate, the thief cannot be charged with the theft of the actual shares. Air, water, gas and electricity can be stolen and charges of theft have resulted from, e.g. the bypassing of an electricity meter.

Property that is not moveable is known as incorporeal property. Incorporeal property, e.g. a person's right to something, cannot be stolen. Problems arise over the theft of information, e.g. computer databases. In *Grant v Allan* (1987) the court held that the accused, making copies of computer print-outs belonging to his employers, may have breached an express or implied obligation to keep material confidential but that it did not amount to criminal conduct.

Human beings cannot be stolen but can be abducted, which is a distinct and separate crime. The exception to this rule relates to prepubescent children. There is the Scots common law crime of child stealing, which is called plagium. This crime can be committed by anyone including a parent who removes their own child, e.g. in contact or residence disputes. Recent cases include *Downie v HM Advocate* (1984) and *Hamilton v Mooney* (1990). In *Downie* the accused was the biological father of a child but was neither married to the child's mother nor did he have custody (now residence) of the child. The jury were charged that in the absence of a custody decree the father of an illegitimate child had no rights to the child and could in theory be convicted of stealing it. If the remains of human beings are stolen from a grave this does not amount to the crime of theft but is the special crime of violation of sepulchres.

Property publicly or privately owned by another person. Things that are not owned are *res nullius* and cannot be stolen. Any property, which is abandoned, is deemed to belong to the Crown. Wild animals are not owned and therefore cannot be stolen, but if they are brought into ownership, e.g. captured and enclosed, they may thereafter be stolen. In *Valentine v Kennedy* (1985) trout which had been purchased from a fish farm were put in an enclosure. The trout escaped from this and were swimming in a burn when the accused and his friends began poaching and caught some fish. The accused were discovered and charged with theft. The trout which had been caught were identified as rainbow trout that had been farmed at the fish farm. The sheriff held that they were still owned, they were capable of being stolen and the accused were convicted of theft.

In *Kane v Friel* (1997) the appellant had been convicted of theft by finding metal piping and a sink. He appealed to the High Court. The police did not see the appellant and his brother taking the property but instead met them, already in possession of the property, crossing waste ground. They told the police they had found the goods and they were going to sell them. At trial, the justice held that they had found the property and appropriated it and also that this property had not been reported as stolen. On appeal, Lord Justice General Rodger noted (at pp.208–209) that, while at common law most abandoned property belongs to the Crown, the advocate-depute did not attempt to find on that "technical doctrine", nor the duties under the Civic Government (Scotland) Act 1982 (s.67), to take care of and deliver property which is found to a police constable or the owner/occupier of the land upon which it is found. Allowing the appeal, Lord Justice General Rodger concluded (at p.210) that the Crown had not proved anything about the circumstances in which the piping or sink were found, there was nothing which would give the justice a basis for inferring that the appellant must have known that the items were property which someone intended to retain and that it was relevant that the items had not been reported stolen.

Erroneous claim of right

If a person takes property in the mistaken belief that it is his or her own, a question would arise as to whether they have the requisite intention to deprive the owner of the property. If these actions result in a charge of theft it is open to an accused to use erroneous claim of right as a defence. The test applied in these circumstances is an objective one, i.e. was the accused's belief both honest and reasonable. It is not enough that the accused believes his actions are not criminal; rather, there must be an erroneous claim of right.

In *Dewar v HM Advocate* (1945) the accused was convicted of the theft of two coffins and the lids of a large number of other coffins. In a statement to the police Dewar admitted the practice of retaining the coffins and said that this was the general practice throughout the crematorium movement. Dewar's position was that upon delivery to the crematorium the coffins and lids were completely under his jurisdiction for disposal. Evidence at the trial demonstrated that this was not the common practice. At trial, the jury were directed on the law relating to erroneous claims of right. The Lord Justice Clerk Cooper directed the jury (at pp.7–8)

> "[to consider] not only the fact that the explanation offered by Dewar was false, and is now admitted to be false, but you will also consider whether he had any colourable ground for holding such a view, or whether the statements made by him to the police ... and other people ... with regard to the practice of the crematorium movement were made recklessly without any justification for belief in their accuracy."

The jury was, therefore, directed to consider whether Dewar's belief was both honest and reasonable. On appeal, Lord Justice General Normand stated (at p.11):

> "It is contrary to the appellant's own evidence that the coffins were completely under his jurisdiction for disposal ... His evidence is a plain assertion of his unlimited right of property in a thing which he knew was sent to him under contract for the purpose of destruction ... Accordingly, in my opinion, there was misappropriation of property which he knew was sent to him merely for destruction by a prescribed method."

Whilst Lord Justice General Normand made it clear that, in his opinion, the trial judge did not require to direct the jury on Dewar's erroneous claim of right, some commentators (e.g. Jones and Christie, 2012, p.167) have not accepted this position. If Dewar honestly believed that he could dispose of the coffins and lids as he pleased, i.e. he was confused as regards the law of property, would he have the requisite mens rea of intention for the crime of theft? Before a belief could negate mens rea it would be tested objectively and requires to be reasonable as well as honest. Whilst a jury may not have accepted that Dewar met this test, the approach adopted by Lord Justice General Normand, namely that there was no need to put Dewar's claim before the jury, is not regarded by commentators as justified.

(3) Without the consent of the owner

This requirement is a means of distinguishing theft from fraud. If an owner agreed to the transfer of goods to the accused, even if the consent is obtained by fraud, then so long as the consent of the owner is clear and is to the permanent appropriation of the goods the crime of theft has not been committed. The actions of the accused may, however, result in another charge, most commonly, fraud. This distinction between theft and fraud is important because a person who purchases an article that was obtained by fraud obtains good title; however, you cannot obtain title to an object that has been stolen (Bell's *Principles*, para.257).

Where an accused has a mistaken belief that the owner consented to the removal of goods, then so long as this belief is both honest and reasonable (an objective test), she will lack the necessary mens rea for the crime of theft.

Mens rea of theft
(4) Intention to deprive the owner of their property
The mens rea of intention in the crime of theft will be inferred from the facts of the case. Until relatively recently, the mens rea of theft was understood to be an intention to deprive permanently an owner of their property. As a consequence, any temporary deprivation was not regarded as theft but the lesser crime of clandestinely taking and using the property of another, e.g. *Strathern v Seaforth* (1926). Recent case law has introduced a more flexible approach to the mens rea of theft but there is a lack of consistency in these decisions. These decisions are discussed under the following headings: intention permanently to deprive; intention to deprive for a nefarious purpose; intention to deprive indefinitely and intention to deprive temporarily.

Intention to deprive permanently. Permanent deprivation refers to where the accused intends to deprive the owner of their property on a permanent basis. The earliest challenge to the accepted rule that permanent deprivation is necessary for the crime of theft is found in *Kivlin v Milne* (1979). In this case the accused was convicted of theft when they took a car without the permission of the owner and left it in a place where the owner was unlikely to find it. No formal opinion was issued but in dismissing the appeal their Lordships said (at p.2) that

> "the learned Sheriff … was entitled to draw the inference that the appellant had the intention permanently to deprive the owner of the motor car of the possession thereof, in that he undoubtedly took possession of it without authority and left the car on each occasion in a place where the owner, by reason of his own investigations, was not liable to discover it."

In this case, the mens rea of theft is still referred to as an intention to permanently deprive the owner of their property. There is, however, some relaxation of the interpretation of permanent and, as a result, the actions of the accused will be held to amount to a permanent deprivation where an owner cannot, on his own investigations, find his property.

Intention to deprive for a nefarious purpose. This form of mens rea has been suggested in cases where the accused withholds property of another until a demand is met. In all reported cases the demand has been for money. In *Milne v Tudhope* (1981) two accused were convicted of the theft of articles they removed from a cottage without the consent of the owner. The accused had been contracted to carry out work on the cottage and, when the owner refused to pay additional monies for remedial work that required to be done, the accused removed radiators, a boiler, etc. which the owner had paid for. On appeal, the High Court held (at p.55) that "a clandestine taking aimed at achieving a nefarious purpose, constitutes theft, even if the taker intends all along to return the thing taken when the purpose has been achieved". The court did stress that it was only in certain exceptional circumstances that an intention to deprive temporarily would suffice.

The approach in *Milne* was followed in *Kidston v Annan* (1984) which involved the accused being convicted of theft as a result of having retained a television set until repairs had been paid for. The owner of the television claimed that he had requested a quote and had not instructed any repairs. In both cases the owner's property was being retained until money was paid to the accused. In *Kidston* the High Court referred to this as holding property to ransom. Such actions have been held to amount to a "nefarious purpose", but this term has also been used in the case *Sandlan v HM Advocate* (1983), which did not involve extortion or property being held to ransom. In *Sandlan* property was removed temporarily, the prosecution claimed, to falsely obtain insurance money. In this case the appellant was a director of the company that the articles were taken from. The second accused, King, gave evidence in his defence, that the goods were only to be removed for a short period so that pilfering by Sandlan would be disguised during stocktaking. Lord Stewart directed the jury that if they accepted King's explanation then the actions of the accused amounted to a nefarious purpose.

This opinion suggests that the court view an intention to deprive for a nefarious purpose necessary before theft can arise from temporary deprivation of property. Later authorities, e.g. *Black v Carmichael*; *Carmichael v Black* (1992), have said that there is no requirement for a "nefarious purpose" even when appropriation is temporary.

Intention to deprive indefinitely. This further development in the mens rea of theft arose in *Fowler v O'Brien* (1994). The appellant was convicted of theft at the district court. He had requested a shot of the complainer's bike and when the latter refused he took the bicycle. The appellant claimed that he told the complainer that he would leave the bicycle at the swimming pool. It is not clear if this was accepted by the justice of the peace but there was evidence that the complainer searched for his bike, including around the swimming pool, and did not recover it for several days. The High Court stated that the facts did not entitle the justice to conclude that there was an intention to permanently or temporarily deprive the owner of their property. The court held (at p.115) that it

> "would be more accurate to say that the owner was indefinitely deprived of their property, since it was not made clear to him whether, and if so, when it would ever be returned to him. In these circumstances there was no need for any clandestine or nefarious purpose to be established. There was no need for any exceptional circumstances. The question is simply whether the necessary criminal intention was present for the taking away of the bicycle to amount to theft. We are persuaded, in the light of the findings, that the justice was entitled to reach the view and to regard this as an act of stealing of the bicycle."

Intention to deprive temporarily. In *Black v Carmichael*; *Carmichael v Black* (1992) the court held that an intention to deprive the owner of their property temporarily will suffice for the crime of theft. Unlike earlier decisions, they do not make reference to temporary deprivation amounting to permanent deprivation (*Kivlin*) nor any requirement for a nefarious purpose to be proven (*Milne, Kidston*). The opinions delivered in this case stress that it is the owner's loss and not the other's gain which is important in relation to the crime of theft.

Dishonest intention to deprive. Two recent cases have suggested that the mens rea of theft requires that an accused has a dishonest intention to deprive the owner of their property. In *Kane v Friel* (1997) (referred to above) the advocate-depute had accepted that the Crown required to prove that the accused must have intended to appropriate the items dishonestly. Lord Justice General Rodger, allowing the appeal, stated:

> "In that situation we are satisfied that there was no sufficient basis on which the justice could infer that the appellant had the necessary dishonest intention to appropriate the copper and the sink. We refer to *Mckenzie v MacLean* [1981], where, in unusual circumstances, the sheriff acquitted the accused on the ground that the Crown had not proved the necessary dishonesty for theft."

This decision has implications for those cases arising from theft by finding.

AGGRAVATED THEFT

The crime of theft can be aggravated by a number of factors that relate to forcing entry to premises so that a theft can be committed. The aggravations are examined below.

THEFT BY OPENING LOCKFAST PLACES

This aggravation involves overcoming the security of anything other than a building. The opening of a lockfast place must precede and be for the purpose of the theft. Examples would include the opening of a parked car, see *McLeod v Mason* (1981). It is unnecessary to specify whether the thief intended to steal the car or something within the car. It is necessary that the car was secure. This crime has been libelled when a stolen bank card obtained during a robbery was used to obtain money from a cash machine (*Johnstone v HM Advocate* (2004)).

THEFT BY HOUSEBREAKING

This aggravation applies when the security of any type of shut and fast roofed building is overcome. Housebreaking includes any action to overcome the security of the building or avoiding the normal obstacles to unauthorised entry, e.g. forcing open a door or window, using a stolen key, entering via a chimney or any other unusual or unauthorised means including using trickery. The housebreaking must precede the theft. Consequently, a thief who hides in a shop and, after it is secured, takes items and breaks out of the shop has not committed an aggravated theft. Similarly, entering a house through an open door or window or turning a key found in a lock would not amount to housebreaking.

The need for a building to be secure and for that security to be overcome before housebreaking is a relevant charge is illustrated by *Lafferty v Wilson* (1990). In *Lafferty* the accused was convicted of housebreaking. This resulted from breaking into an unoccupied flat in November 1988. Before July 1988 this flat had been the subject of a number of housebreakings. On appeal, the conviction was quashed as it could not be proven, first, that the flat was secure prior to the accused gaining entry and, secondly, that the accused had overcome the security of the building.

HOUSEBREAKING WITH INTENT TO STEAL

This aggravation is charged when the accused unsuccessfully attempts the crime of theft by housebreaking (*Burns v Allan* (1987)). Housebreaking with intent to commit a crime other than theft is not a crime in itself (*HM Advocate v Forbes* (1994)).

ROBBERY

Where theft is accomplished by personal violence or intimidation, it is the crime of robbery. The violence used need not amount to an assault. As theft is an essential element of robbery, the law relating to theft, namely the mens rea and the actus reus, apply equally to robbery. The caveat to this is that robbery will always involve taking rather than appropriation of goods already in the possession of the accused. This is because robbery requires the violent removal of goods from the victim. The goods do not need to belong to the victim; it is enough if the victim is acting as a custodian. In *Flynn v HM Advocate* (1995) the appellant and another man were charged with assault and robbery. There was no evidence that the appellant had been responsible for any violence. The jury returned a verdict of not proven in respect of the assault charge subject to a deletion of "seize him by the throat, repeatedly punch him on the face whereby he fell to the ground" and a verdict of guilty of robbery. This conviction was appealed on the ground that a conviction of robbery was perverse where all reference to violence had been deleted. The court held that where an indictment libels a charge of robbery and details the violence used, the jury are not entitled to convict of robbery where they have deleted reference to the accused being responsible for any violence either on his own or while acting art and part. The verdict of robbery in this case was set aside and a verdict of theft substituted. The court observed that it would be competent to bring a charge of robbery without specifying the violence used. It should be noted that *Flynn* involved an accused acting in concert with another and, subsequently, the courts have taken a different approach when the accused has acted alone when carrying out a robbery. In the recent case of *Rory v HM Advocate* (2010) the accused was charged with assault and robbery. The complainer, whose memory of the incident was poor, said in evidence that he had been "mugged", and that there was "a lot of scuffling" but did not speak to the specific assaults libelled. The jury convicted the appellant of robbery under deletion of the reference to assault in the first charge of robbery and the narrative of the assault in the second charge of assault. He appealed on the ground that the conviction should have been one of theft, given the deletion of violence from the robbery charge. The court held that in the circumstances violence was used to obtain control of the complainer's property, that the violence was sufficient as an ingredient in robbery, and that there was nothing inconsistent in the verdict and appeal was refused. Similarly, in *Morrison v HM Advocate* (2010) the jury deleted reference to assault in their verdict. The Appeal Court held that the appellant's actions in leading the complainer to an alley then scuffling with him prior to stealing money and a mobile phone demonstrated violence by the appellant which was used to obtain control of the complainer's property and could not be described as *de minimis*. In both *Rory* and *Morrison* neither complainer could recall the details of the violence used.

Any degree of violence or intimidation is sufficient so long as it is for the purpose of stealing the property (*MacKay v HM Advocate* (1997)).

This violence does not need to involve wounding or beating. In *Cromar v HM Advocate* (1987) the accused came up behind the complainer and pulled at a bag of money he was holding until the handle snapped. The accused appealed against his conviction of robbery on the basis that he should only have been charged with theft as he only pulled the bag once.

The court held that there was sufficient evidence to entitle the jury to reach the conclusion that theft had been accomplished by personal violence and that, therefore, the crime was robbery.

Intimidation may consist of any threat of immediate injury that induces the victim to hand over the property. Violence that occurs after seizing property does not amount to robbery and in these circumstances the appropriate charges are assault and theft.

The doctrine of recent possession (see p.80 of this text) has been held to apply to robbery despite the fact that mere possession of property is incapable of proving that violence or intimidation was involved in the removal of the property from its owner.

EMBEZZLEMENT

The crime of embezzlement involves a dishonest failure to account for goods entrusted to the accused. The accused will not only have had possession of the goods but also the power to undertake transactions as if the property was his own. The actus reus requires an unauthorised act on the part of the accused and the mens rea can be described as a dishonest and felonious intent to appropriate the property of another. Evidence of dishonesty is necessary (*Allenby v HM Advocate* (1938), *Moore v HM Advocate* (2010)).

The mens rea and actus reus of theft and embezzlement are, therefore, very similar, namely intention and appropriation. Differences between the two crimes are more difficult to identify. One such difference is that whilst incorporeal property cannot be stolen it can be embezzled (*Guild v Lees* (1994)). An interesting difference is that professional people who appropriate goods in their trust embezzle whereas non-professional people steal (*Edgar v MacKay* (1926)). The ability to distinguish between the two crimes is now of less importance, as it is competent to return a conviction of theft on a charge of embezzlement and vice versa (CPSA 1995 Sch.3). Furthermore, it is now competent to return a verdict of fraud on a charge of embezzlement and vice versa (CJLSA 2010 s.36).

FRAUD

Fraud was defined by Macdonald as the "bringing about of any practical result by false pretences" (Macdonald, p.52).

The actus reus of fraud requires a false pretence, a practical result and a causal link between the false pretence and the practical result. The mens rea requires that the accused acted intentionally with the knowledge that the pretence was false. The completed crime requires that the third party is deceived and acts in a way they would not otherwise have done without the false pretence. Fraud is a result crime.

Actus reus of fraud
A false pretence
The false pretence can be express or implied and may result from either positive actions or a failure to do something. An express action has been held to include where the accused misrepresents the value of work done to property (*HM Advocate v McAllister* (1996)), the necessity for or extent of roof repairs together with overcharging (*McPhee v HM Advocate* (2009), *Cummings v HM Advocate* (2009)) and an implied action, where animals being displayed at a prize show were made more attractive (*James Paton* (1858)). A failure to disclose relevant information to the rating authorities was held to be sufficient for the actus reus of fraud in *Strathern v Fogal* (1922). Where false representations were made in respect of a future intention, this was held to amount to fraud in *Richards v HM Advocate* (1971).

Practical result
The result of the false pretence will be dependent on the type of pretence. The important factor is that the victim must have acted in a way that they would not otherwise have done without the false pretence. There must be a causal link between the pretence and the practical result (*Mather v HM Advocate* (1914)).

Mens rea of fraud
The mens rea of fraud necessitates that the accused knew that the pretence was false and intended to deceive the other party. Any charge must state that the party knew that their representation was false. In *Bennett v Houston* (1993) a conviction of fraud was quashed on appeal because of a fatal defect in each charge as it failed to narrate that the truth, as the accused well knew, was that the true value of works undertaken was not the sum that he claimed to be the value. An honest and reasonable belief in the truth of the statement will vitiate the charge of fraud.

Recklessness is not recognised as sufficient for the mens rea of fraud. In *Mackenzie v Skeen* (1971) the accused was extremely careless when he weighed offal that was to be sold to pet food manufacturers. In the absence of an intention to deceive either his employer or the owner of the pet food company he was acquitted of fraud.

RESET

Hume defined reset as "the receiving and keeping of stolen goods, knowing them to be such, and with an intention to conceal and withhold them from the owner" (I, 113). Whilst reset was originally limited to the retention of those goods obtained by theft or robbery, this has now been extended to include goods obtained by fraud, embezzlement and breach of trust (Criminal Law (Consolidation) (Scotland) Act 1995 s.51). The actus reus of reset is the retention of goods obtained dishonestly and the mens rea is knowledge of the origin of the goods and the intention to withhold the property from the true owner. It is not possible to be convicted of the theft and reset of the same property. Nevertheless, it is competent to return a verdict of guilty of reset on a charge of theft. A conviction of theft cannot be returned on a charge of reset because the former is a more serious crime.

Actus reus

Hume and subsequent case law stated that the actus reus of reset required that the accused take possession of the goods. Any period of possession, however slight, is sufficient (*Robert Finlay* (1826)). The crime is committed at the point of receipt of the goods. It is not necessary for the accused to intend to retain the goods permanently. The actual goods must be retained and retention of the proceeds from the sale of the goods does not amount to reset. Retention can occur either from purchasing the goods or retaining them on behalf of a third party on a gratuitous basis. It is not necessary for the accused to receive the goods directly from the thief. Where stolen property has been passed amongst a number of individuals it may be more difficult to prove the requisite mens rea for each to be found guilty of reset.

Contrary to the views of Hume and others, Macdonald suggests that the crime of reset can be committed where an accused is "privy to the retaining of property that has been dishonestly come by" (p.67). This removes the necessity that the accused has taken possession of the goods. In *HM Advocate v Browne* (1903) (at p.26) Lord Justice Clerk Kinsburgh (Macdonald) directed a jury that:

> "If a man steals a bundle of notes out of a man's pocket and after that informs another man that he has got these notes … or if the man saw him stealing them and knew they were stolen, then if the other man connived at it remaining in the possession of the thief or being out in any place for safe custody, such as hiding in a cupboard, he is guilty of receiving feloniously even although he never puts his fingers on the notes at all."

It is not clear from the reported cases what is required for connivance, but *Browne* suggests that it may be inferred from inactivity on the part of the accused. While this has been followed in some cases, e.g. *McNeil v HM Advocate* (1968), it has been questioned in others. In *Clark v HM Advocate* (1965) Lord Justice Clerk Grant held that the sheriff's direction that connivance could be inferred from mere inactivity on the part of the accused was incorrect. In *Hipson v Tudhope* (1983) Lord Justice Clerk Wheatley said (at p.660):

> "The only point at issue is whether there was evidence which warranted the sheriff arriving at the decision … that the appellant was privy to the retention of the stolen car so as to constitute the crime of reset … All the appellant said when he was cautioned and charged

was simply 'not guilty'. In that situation ... I am of [the] opinion that the situation clearly falls into the category that was recognised in *Clark v HM Advocate* ... as being a situation where an inference of guilty knowledge could not be gathered from the mere silence of the accused."

Mens rea

The mens rea of reset is knowledge that the goods have been obtained dishonestly and an intention to deprive the owner of the goods. Knowledge of the source of goods can be difficult to establish. It is not enough for an accused to say that they did not appreciate the source of goods, and where an accused "wilfully blinds himself" to the origin of goods this will not act as a defence to a charge of reset (*Latta v Herron* (1967)). If an accused honestly and reasonably believes that goods are from an honest source she will lack the requisite mens rea for the crime of reset.

An evidential rule that assists in proving the mens rea of both reset and theft is the doctrine of recent possession. The doctrine is that an inference of guilt can be drawn from an accused being in possession of recently stolen property in *criminative* circumstances (*Davidson v Brown* (1990)). The mens rea of reset can also be inferred from the accused's account of how she came to be in possession of goods. If an accused provides an awkward explanation of how she came to be in possession of stolen goods, the jury are entitled to infer from this that the accused had the knowledge necessary for the crime of reset (*Forbes v HM Advocate* (1995)). As noted previously, this doctrine has been held to also apply to robbery.

Wife's privilege

Traditionally in Scots law a wife could not be convicted of reset of property stolen by her husband. This approach was varied in the case *Smith v Watson* (1982) where a wife was convicted of the reset of money that her husband had obtained in a robbery. The money was posted through her letterbox while her husband was in prison, having already been convicted of the robbery from which the money was the proceeds. The court held that the money was not being retained to protect or shield the husband but for his subsequent use on his release from prison. In these circumstances, the wife's privilege was held not to apply.

UTTERING AS GENUINE

Forgery is not a crime at common law unless the forgery is "uttered", i.e. presented to a third party as genuine. It is necessary that the perpetrator knows that the document is forged and intends that the other party should be deceived by it. A practical result is not necessary (see Hume, I, 148–149 and *Burke v MacPhail* (1984)).

OFFENCES AGAINST PROPERTY

In this section the crimes of malicious mischief, vandalism and fire-raising will be considered.

MALICIOUS MISCHIEF

Malicious mischief is the intentional or reckless damage of property without the owner's consent. The property must belong to another person. Hume's definition of this crime required physical damage to the property and some element of civil disturbance. However, the current law no longer requires any civil disturbance (*Ward v Robertson* (1938)) and the definition of damage to property has been extended to include patrimonial loss caused by the actions of the accused (*HM Advocate v Wilson* (1984)).

In *Wilson* the accused was charged with malicious mischief when he pressed the emergency button of a turbine at a power station which resulted in electricity to the value of £147,000 having to be replaced from other sources. The accused was acquitted at trial and the Crown appealed to the High Court. In his report to the High Court the sheriff stated (at p.117):

> "My reason for holding the indictment irrelevant ... is that hitherto the crime of malicious mischief has necessarily involved some physical damage or injury to property ... It is not libelled that any physical damage was done to the generator. It may be desirable that the law should regard as criminal any wilful or reckless act which causes financial loss, but hitherto that has not been understood by the law."

The Lord Justice Clerk (Lord Wheatley, at p.119), held that the crime of malicious mischief

> "has to be a deliberate and malicious act to damage another's property, or to interfere with it to the detriment of the owner or lawful possessor ... This leaves for consideration only the question whether what resulted from this initial act was 'damage' or 'patrimonial loss' ... In my opinion, the occurrence has to be looked at as a whole. If the malicious intention improperly to stop the production of electricity is established, and the achievement of that had the effect of rendering inoperative a machine which should have been operating productively and profitably, then in my view that is just as much damage to the employer's property as would be the case in any of the more physical acts of sabotage."

His Lordship concluded that the crime libelled fell within Hume's definition of malicious mischief. Lord McDonald agreed with Lord Wheatley, but Lord Stewart dissented stating (at p.122):

"This is not in my view, merely a case where the modus of an established crime may change with changing circumstances. Rather is it a case where an essential constituent of the crime is seen to be missing from the libel. I do not consider that the failure of a machine to operate through being switched off can be equated to the failure of a machine to be able to operate through being destroyed or damaged … I consider that actual destruction or damage is an essential of the crime."

The approach in *Wilson* has been confirmed in *Bett v Hamilton* (1997). However, a limit has been placed on what qualifies as patrimonial loss. In *Bett* the accused was convicted of malicious mischief when he changed the angle of a bank security camera. It was suggested that the costs of running the security camera were wasted and that there was an increased risk of housebreaking, theft or vandalism. Lord Sutherland delivered the opinion of the court, at pp.623 to 624:

"What is required in such a charge [malicious mischief] is that there should be a wilful intent to cause injury to the owner or possessor of the property. This injury may either be in the form of physical damage or in the form of patrimonial loss. We do not consider that the matters referred to by the advocate-depute properly constitute patrimonial loss. The running costs of the camera would have been incurred in any event, even if it had been pointing in the right direction, and accordingly what has been lost to the bank is such benefit as they may have obtained from the fact that the camera was pointing in the correct direction … The bank on these averments suffered no financial loss whatsoever and therefore there is no patrimonial loss."

Where an accused damages the property of another in the belief that he is legally justified, this will not act as a defence (*Clark v Syme* (1957)). This applies even where the accused acts on the basis of vindication of rights, i.e. that an individual may damage another person's property in order to protect their own property rights.

VANDALISM

Vandalism is the statutory equivalent to malicious mischief. The offence was created in 1980 and the current law is contained within s.52 of the Criminal Law (Consolidation) (Scotland) Act 1995. This section states that "any person who, without reasonable excuse, wilfully or recklessly destroys or damages any property belonging to another shall be guilty of the offence of vandalism". The mens rea required is either intention or recklessness. One difference between vandalism and malicious mischief is that the former requires that the damage or destruction be done "without reasonable excuse". Where an accused presents a "reasonable excuse" the onus is on the prosecution to prove that the excuse is not reasonable (*MacDougal v Yuk-Sun Ho* (1985)).

FIRE-RAISING

The crime of fire-raising is a serious form of malicious mischief. Traditionally this was a capital offence where the property burned was houses, corn, coal heughs, woods and under-woods (Hume, I, 31). Fire-raising involves the intentional or reckless damaging or destroying of corporeal property belonging to another without his consent or permission. The crime of fire-raising traditionally took three forms: wilful fire-raising, intentional fire-raising and reckless fire-raising. Now two forms of fire-raising are recognised by the courts, namely wilful fire-raising and reckless fire-raising. Either crime can be committed in respect of any type of property (*Byrne v HM Advocate* (2000)).

Wilful fire-raising
Wilful fire-raising requires that the accused intentionally set fire to property. The mens rea, therefore, is intention and the actus reus is the setting fire to the property of another.

Before an accused can be convicted of wilful fire-raising in respect of any particular item of property, the Crown must establish beyond reasonable doubt that she intended to set fire to that item of property. This becomes more complex where an accused intends to set fire to an item within a property and unintentionally the fire spreads to the whole building. Such a scenario occurred in the case of *Blane v HM Advocate* (1991) where the accused set fire to a quilt in a room within a hostel. He gave evidence that he did this so that he could inhale the smoke and thereby commit suicide. He neither intended nor foresaw that the fire would spread as it did causing £15,000 worth of damage. On appeal, the court held that a conviction of wilful fire-raising required that the accused intended to set fire to the building or showed an utter disregard from which his intention could be inferred. This reference to utter disregard, i.e. a high degree of recklessness, as being equivalent to intention was subsequently overruled by *Byrne v HM Advocate* (2000).

In *Byrne* a bench of five judges confirmed that the crime of wilful fire-raising requires a mens rea of intention and that no degree of recklessness will be treated as equivalent to intent. They also said that there was no place for the doctrine of transferred intention in the crime of fire-raising (see Ch.2). The charges of wilful and reckless fire-raising are not inter-changeable as they have different mens rea, so it is not possible to convict of one crime on a charge of the other. If the prosecution wish to have the option of either wilful or reckless fire-raising, it is necessary that both charges appear as alternatives on the indictment. Where there are alternative charges, a verdict of guilty can only be returned in respect of one of the charges.

Reckless fire-raising
This crime involves recklessly setting fire to the property of another. The crime is not restricted to particular types of property. Reckless fire-raising could be charged, for example, if an accused set fire to his own property and this spread to an adjoining property. This crime requires that the perpetrator had a mens rea of recklessness at the point at which the fire was started. It is not enough that the fire was started accidentally and thereafter the accused failed to take steps to contain or put the fire out (*McCue v Currie* (2004) discussed in Ch.2).

READING

T. Jones and M. Christie, *Criminal Law*, 5th edn (Edinburgh: W. Green & Son, 2012), Chs 10 and 11.
C. Gane, C. Stoddart and J. Chalmers, *A Casebook on Scottish Criminal Law*, 4th edn (Edinburgh: W. Green & Son, 2009), Chs 11–15.
G.H. Gordon, *Criminal Law*, edited by M. Christie, 3rd edn (Edinburgh: W. Green & Son, 2001), Vol. II.

5. CRIMES RELATING TO PUBLIC ORDER

Offences against public order include breach of the peace and mobbing. In this chapter, offences against the state will also be considered.

BREACH OF THE PEACE

Until the decision of the Appeal Court in *Smith (P) v Donnelly* (2001) the actus reus of breach of the peace was so widely defined that it was suggested that almost all of the criminal law of Scotland could fall within the definition. The court in *Smith* observed that breach of the peace can be committed in a wide variety of circumstances and that a comprehensive definition which would cover all of these is neither possible nor desirable. The Appeal Court held that the actus reus of breach of the peace required conduct severe enough to cause alarm to ordinary people and threaten serious disturbance to the community. (This is referred to as the "conjunctive test" and was confirmed in *Harris v HM Advocate* (2009), *W.M. v HM Advocate* (2010) and *Anoliefo v HM Advocate* (2012)). Something greater than irritation was required and the conduct should be genuinely alarming and disturbing, in its context, to any reasonable person. Furthermore, a breach of the peace could be committed in public or private. A bench of five judges subsequently confirmed the approach adopted by the Appeal Court in *Smith (P) v Donnelly* (2001) (*Jones v Carnegie*; *Tallents v Gallacher*; *Barret v Carnegie*; *Carberry v Currie*; *Park v Frame* (2004)). The European Court of Human Rights held that the definition of the offence of breach of the peace as stipulated in *Smith (P) v Donnelly* (2001) is sufficiently precise to provide reasonable forseeability of the actions which may fall within the remit of the offence (*Lucas v United Kingdom* (2003)).

It is clear that the mens rea of breach of the peace is not intention or recklessness. In *Hughes v Crowe* (1993) the court held that the mens rea of breach of the peace should be inferred from the nature and quality of the acts complained of. In *Hughes* the accused was charged with breach of the peace as a result of playing loud music and making noise in his flat between 7.15am and 8.15am on a Saturday morning. This had disturbed the occupants of the flat below. The noise, the time of day and the location of his flat in close proximity to others were held to be relevant circumstances as was the fact that the accused's conduct was deliberate.

The assumption that breach of the peace could be committed in private has now been removed. In the leading case of *Harris v HM Advocate* (2009) a bench of five judges who held that the true nature of breach of the peace is that it is a crime that has at least a public element and the offending conduct should, in some sense at least, cause or threaten disturbance to the public peace, and that absent a public element the offence was not committed.

Acts, which are in themselves both lawful and unlawful, may be regarded as a breach of the peace. Whilst this crime was commonly charged in Scots law in response to incidents of domestic abuse that occur in private, the effect of *Harris* and the demand for a public element now excludes such behaviours from the ambit of breach of the peace. This has resulted in the inclusion of an offence of "threatening and abusive behaviour" in s.38 of the CJLSA 2010. Section 38 defines this offence as involving behaviour that is threatening or abusive which is likely to cause the reasonable person fear or alarm. The perpetrator must either intend to cause fear or alarm or be reckless as to whether their behaviour would have such an effect. It is a defence if the perpetrator can show that their behaviour was reasonable in the particular circumstances. Behaviour includes things said or otherwise communicated as well as things done in a single act or a course of conduct. Section 39 of said Act introduces an offence of "stalking". Behaviour amounting to stalking was previously prosecuted as breach of the peace in Scotland.

MOBBING

Mobbing is committed by being part of a mob who act together with a common illegal purpose. The mens rea of mobbing is not dealt with explicitly in any cases. However, it clearly demands knowledge of the common purpose that is being pursued. The actus reus of mobbing has three elements: (1) there must be a number of people; (2) there must be a common illegal purpose; and (3) the conduct of the mob must cause public alarm and disturbance. The similarity between the crime of mobbing and the requirements of art and part liability is obvious. Where there is a common purpose to commit a particular crime then it would be competent to charge the accused art and part with that crime. For example, if in the course of mobbing a death results it is competent to charge the accused art and part with the crime of murder or, alternatively, mobbing. In this scenario the former is more likely as murder is a more serious crime attracting a mandatory life sentence.

Actus reus
(1) There must be a number of people
There is no specified minimum or maximum number of people required for mobbing, although eight has been deemed to be an acceptable number (*Hancock v HM Advocate* (1981)) and there has been a suggestion that five may be too few (*Sloan v MacMillan* (1922)).

(2) There must be a common illegal purpose
A peaceful and legal common purpose would not fulfil the requirements of mobbing, instead the common purpose must be a violent or mischievous one (*Alexander McLean* (1886)). The common purpose does not require to be planned but can arise spontaneously, e.g. a peaceful and legal demonstration which becomes one involving a common illegal purpose (*George Smith* (1848)).

(3) Conduct of the mob must cause public alarm and disturbance

The conduct of the mob must cause significant public alarm and disturbance (Hume, I, 416).

OFFENCES AGAINST THE STATE

This group of offences does not have an official title. They include: treason, sedition, perjury, attempt to pervert the course of justice and giving false information to the authorities.

TREASON

This offence is only of importance in wartime or in time of rebellion. The offence involves a violation of allegiance to the government and the Crown. Offences against state security in peace time are generally not regarded as treason but as specific statutory offences, e.g. breach of the Official Secrets Acts 1911–1989.

SEDITION

The crime of sedition was abolished by s.37A of the CJLSA 2010.

PERJURY

This common law crime involves the judicial affirmation of falsehood upon oath (Hume, I, 369). So, if a witness lies under oath she can be convicted of perjury if the evidence she gave was pertinent to the point at issue. The actus reus of the offence is the giving of the evidence and the mens rea is the knowledge that it is not true (*HM Advocate v Sheridan (Thomas)*, 2012 S.C.L. 298).

ATTEMPT TO PERVERT OR DEFEAT OR HINDER THE COURSE OF JUSTICE

Note these are completed crimes and not criminal attempts. The word "attempt" is used in a descriptive rather than a legal sense. The mens rea is intention to pervert the course of justice.

GIVING FALSE INFORMATION TO THE AUTHORITIES

This could be classified as an attempt to pervert the course of justice but,

as it normally involves information at the beginning of an investigation
rather than contributing to an investigation which is on-going, the tendency
is to charge it as a crime in its own right. The crime takes two forms:

(1)   Making a false accusation of crime against a particular named
        individual.
(2)   Giving of false information to the police or procurator fiscal which
        results in an investigation. This is sometimes referred to as wasting
        police time. The mens rea is intention and knowledge that the
        information is false.

READING

T. Jones and M. Christie, *Criminal Law*, 5th edn (Edinburgh: W. Green &
    Son, 2012), Ch.12.
C. Gane, C. Stoddart and J. Chalmers, *A Casebook on Scottish Criminal
    Law*, 4th edn (Edinburgh: W. Green & Son, 2009), Ch.16.
G.H. Gordon, *Criminal Law*, edited by M. Christie, 3rd edn (Edinburgh: W.
    Green & Son, 2001), Vol. II.

6. DEFENCES

Criminal defences are an essential element of any legal system. Defences can result in an accused being acquitted or, alternatively, their criminal responsibility being mitigated.

Criminal defences operate in one of three ways. First, they may justify the accused's behaviour and result in acquittal. Even though the prosecution has proved each element in the definition of the crime, these are often referred to as justifying defences and would include self-defence, coercion and necessity.

Secondly, there are defences that operate to excuse the actions of the accused. In such cases, the elements of the definition of the crime have been proved by the prosecution but, because of some excusing condition, the accused cannot be held fully responsible for her actions. Excuses are recognised where the accused has committed an unjustifiable act but cannot be regarded as morally blameworthy, e.g. an accused who pleads mental disorder to a charge of murder does not claim that she was justified in killing but rather that she is not morally blameworthy due to her mental condition. These defences are often referred to as excuses and include mental disorder and provocation. Note that some excusing defences will result in acquittal, e.g. mental disorder, or will mitigate the crime, e.g. from murder to culpable homicide in the case of provocation.

Thirdly, a defence may raise a reasonable doubt concerning a material element of the prosecution's case, e.g. the defence of alibi establishes that the accused did not in fact perpetuate the actus reus of the crime.

Note that, as well as these formal methods of mitigating responsibility, a plea in mitigation may be presented to the court on behalf of the accused. This will take place after the accused has either pled or been found guilty and is done with the purpose of lessening the punishment given. An accused is also entitled to introduce evidence of mitigating circumstances in the course of his trial.

SPECIAL DEFENCES

Criminal defences are not only distinguished by the ways in which they operate but also in the procedure attached to them in court. The term "special defence" is a procedural term and refers to the defences which an accused is not allowed to state unless written notice has been lodged in advance of the preliminary hearing or before the first diet (CPSA 1995 s.79), except where the accused is able to satisfy the court that there was good reason for not having done so. Similar requirements apply to summary proceedings. This requirement applies to the special defences of alibi, incrimination, mental disorder and self-defence as well as the other defences of automatism, coercion and consent in sexual offences. In addition to sharing procedural rules, special defences are those which Lord

Walker in *Adam v Macneill* (1972) said "put in issue a fact (1) which is not referred to in the libel, and (2) which, if established, necessarily results in acquittal of the accused". Note that acquittal can also result from the defence of necessity but this defence does not require to be notified to the court before the trial. The new disclosure requirements introduced by ss.124 and 125 of the CJLSA 2010 state that in solemn proceedings an accused must lodge a defence statement at least 14 days before the first diet stating the nature of the accused's defence, including any particular defences on which the accused intends to rely. An accused may lodge a defence statement in summary proceedings after a plea of not guilty has been recorded but this is not mandatory.

(1) Alibi
This defence is simply that at the time of the offence the accused was not at the place libelled. If such a defence is lodged it must be relevant and, therefore, specify where the accused was, and at what time.

(2) Incrimination
The defence of incrimination involves a claim that the crime was not committed by the accused but by another person, who is named if they are known. It is not a special defence where the accused attempts to incriminate his co-accused. In this instance, however, notice of intention to lead evidence to support such a claim must be lodged with the court (s.78 of the CPSA 1995).

(3) Mental disorder
Mental disorder (previously known as insanity) is used in pleadings in criminal law in two ways. First, it is used as a plea in bar of trial and, secondly, as a special defence. Replacing the term "insanity" with mental disorder reflects the facts that the term insanity had no medical meaning and was previously defined by case law (*Brennan v HM Advocate* (1977). In addition to the term insanity being replaced by "mental disorder", the test for unfitness for trial now includes both physical and mental conditions. The "tests" for unfitness for trial and mental disorder are now defined in s.53F and s.51A respectively of the CPSA 1995 (as inserted by s.168 of the CJLSA 2010).

Unfitness for trial
This is not a special defence but will normally be a preliminary plea, i.e. a plea that is heard before the trial commences, to prevent the trial proceeding because the accused is unfit for trial. Notice of such a preliminary plea requires to be given in accordance with s.71(2) of the CPSA 1995. The test used to determine if an accused is unfit for trial is contained in s.53F of the CPSA 1995. A person will be held to be unfit for trial if it is established on the balance of probabilities that the person is incapable, by reason of mental or physical condition, of participating effectively in a trial. In determining this question, the court is to have regard to the person's ability to:

(a)   understand the nature of the charge;
(b)   understand the requirement to tender a plea to the charge and the effect of such a plea;
(c)   understand the purpose of, and follow the course of, the trial;
(d)   understand the evidence that may be given against the person;
(e)   instruct or otherwise communicate with the person's legal representative; and
(f)   understand any other factors which the court considers relevant.

These tests are applied at the time the trial is to take place rather than when an offence was alleged to have been committed. The previous requirement for supporting oral or written evidence from two medical practitioners has been repealed. Section 53F(3) states that inability to recall events is not a sufficient ground upon which to find an accused unfit to plead.

If an accused is found unfit for trial, instead of a trial there is an "examination of the facts". Section 55 of the CPSA 1995 states that, at an examination of the facts, the court shall, on the basis of evidence given, determine whether it is satisfied beyond reasonable doubt that: (i) the accused committed the offence charged; and (ii) on the balance of probabilities that there are no grounds for acquitting her. The court may also (iii) acquit the person on the grounds that they suffered from a mental disorder when they committed the offence. If any of these conclusions are reached, the following methods of disposal are open to the court:

(a)   a compulsion order;
(b)   in addition to a compulsion order, make a restriction order;
(bb) make an interim compulsion order;
(c)   make a guardianship order placing the person under the guardianship of the local authority;
(d)   make a supervision and treatment order; or
(e)   make no order.

Mental disorder as a defence

The mental disorder defence (previously known as insanity) differs from the plea in bar of trial. As it is a special defence, the accused must give the court notice that the defence will be pled at least seven days before the preliminary hearing in a solemn trial or before the first diet in summary proceedings (s.78(3) of the CPSA 1995). The defence is pled in the course of a normal trial and the only variation on normal procedure is that the onus of proof switches to the defence, but only for the purpose of proving the mental disorder defence.

What is required for the mental disorder defence?

If at the time of the conduct constituting an offence a person was unable by reason of mental disorder to appreciate the nature or wrongfulness of the conduct, that person is not criminally responsible for conduct constituting an offence (CPSA 1995 s.51A as amended by s.168 of the CJLSA 2010).

The two requirements of this complete defence are that the accused was suffering from a mental disorder at the time the act was committed and that she was "unable to appreciate the nature or wrongfulness of her conduct".

Much of the previous case law relating to the insanity defence can still be relied upon since the 2010 Act mostly codifies the law as it stood. The leading case on insanity was *Brennan v HM Advocate* (1977). Any mental disorder must have an internal cause and it is this which distinguishes it from automatism. It should be noted that mental disorder does not include a personality disorder which is characterised solely or principally by abnormally aggressive or seriously irresponsible conduct (CPSA s.51A(2)). The requirement that the accused appreciated the nature of the conduct refers to moral rather than legal wrongfulness of the conduct involved.

Burden of proof

Where mental disorder is pled the burden of proof lies on the accused in respect of proving mental disorder. The standard of proof required is, however, lower than for the prosecution. Whereas the latter must prove beyond reasonable doubt that the accused committed the crime charged, the defence of mental disorder requires to be proven on the balance of probabilities. As with insanity, mental disorder is a matter for the jury to determine.

Intoxication and mental disorder

Regarding the question of whether mental disorder could be induced by drugs and alcohol guidance is available from *Brennan v HM Advocate* (1977). This appeal was decided by a bench of seven judges. Rejecting the first ground of appeal they said (at p.153):

> "In short, insanity in our law requires proof of total alienation of reason in relation to the act charged as the result of mental illness, mental disease or defect or unsoundness of mind and does not comprehend the malfunctioning or transitory effect, as the result of deliberate and self-induced intoxication."

The second ground of appeal was that the appellant was intoxicated to such a degree that he was deprived of all capacity to form the "specific intent" which is of the essence of the crime of murder. The court reiterated that self-induced intoxication, whatever the degree, is not insanity (now mental disorder) and cannot support a defence of diminished responsibility, and that in these areas the law of Scotland is consistent with Hume and Alison (at p.155) that "self-induced intoxication is no defence to any criminal charge, at least for an offence in itself perilous or hurtful".

Disposal and mental disorder

Where a person is acquitted on the grounds of his mental disorder, at the time of the act or omission, the court will dispose of the case using the provisions of s.57 of the 1995 Act, previously listed.

(4) Self-defence
Self-defence is available where an accused intentionally uses physical force
to protect herself, or others (*HM Advocate v Carson* (1964); *Dewar v HM
Advocate* (2009)), from an attack. Self-defence is therefore pled in response
to a charge of assault or murder. The rules are the same in both contexts,
except that where self-defence is used in response to an assault, there does
not need to be imminent danger of death but merely imminent danger of
serious injury. As self-defence can serve to justify a fatal attack on another
person it is not surprising that the rules of this defence are rather restricted.
In the case of homicide the essential elements are set out in *HM Advocate
v Doherty* (1954):

- The accused must be in imminent danger to life.
- The accused must use any reasonable opportunity to escape but
  would not be required to put himself at greater risk (*McBrearty v
  HM Advocate* (1999)). In cases where the accused is acting in
  defence of another there is no requirement to use any reasonable
  means of escape but the use of violence must be unavoidable
  (*Dewar v HM Advocate* (2009); *Fitzpatrick v HM Advocate* (1992)).
- The degree of violence used in self-defence must be proportionate
  to the attack and not excessive (*Moore v MacDougall* (1989)).

The requirements are, therefore, that any threat to life must be imminent
and, therefore, threats of future injury will not be enough. Secondly, if there
is a reasonable means of escape then the individual is under a duty to use
it, unless they are acting to protect a third party. Thirdly, the force used
must be both necessary in the circumstances and also proportional to the
threat. In *Fenning v HM Advocate* (1985) Lord Cameron said (at p.225):

> "While the law permits the use of force in repelling force when escape
> from the attacker is not reasonably possible, the protection which the
> law affords to the victim of an attack is not a licence to use force
> grossly in excess of that necessary to defend himself ... That is the
> foundation on which the plea itself is based. What is that excess in a
> particular case is a matter for the jury to decide on the evidence before
> them and under proper and sufficient direction in law."

The issue of proportionate retaliation is complex. Directions to juries have,
however, shed some light on the requirements. In *HM Advocate v Doherty*
(1954) the accused was charged with the culpable homicide of a man called
Cairns, by stabbing him in the eye with a bayonet. A means of escape
existed at the time so that retreat would have been possible. A special
defence of self-defence was lodged by the accused. Doherty claimed that
he killed Cairns while defending himself from a hammer attack. On the
question of proportionate retaliation, Lord Keith directed the jury (at
pp.4–5):

"You do not need an exact proportion of injury and retaliation; it is not a matter that you weigh in too fine scales ... Some allowance must be made for the excitement or the state of fear or the heat of blood at the moment of the man who is attacked, but there are limits or tests that are perfectly well recognised that will help you to understand this doctrine by way of illustration. For instance, if a man was struck a blow by another man with the fist, that could not justify retaliation by the use of a knife, because there is no real proportion at all between a blow with a fist and retaliation by a knife, and therefore, you have got to consider this question of proportion between the attack made and the retaliation offered."

The terms of this direction continue to be used, e.g. *Lucas v HM Advocate* (2010). Where it is clear from the evidence that an accused has acted with excessive force that went far beyond any measures reasonably required, the trial judge will have a duty to withdraw self-defence from the jury (*Pollock v HM Advocate* (1998)).

Self-defence and rape
The exception to the requirement that an accused must be in imminent danger of life before self-defence can be pled is where a woman is resisting an attack of rape (*Pollock v HM Advocate* (1998)). As noted in Ch.3, under Scots common law rape was a crime that could only be committed against a woman, but the Sexual Offences (Scotland) Act 2009 s.1 now defines rape victims as either men or women, although the perpetrators can still only be men. As a consequence of the common law definition, retaliation to an attack of rape was only available to a woman, or people assisting her to resist an attack, and was not extended to men defending themselves from an attack of sodomy (*McCluskey v HM Advocate* (1959)). Given the change in the definition of the crime of rape, one would expect self-defence to now be available to men responding to an attack of rape.

Mistaken belief and self-defence
The question of mistaken belief and self-defence will arise where an accused mistakenly believes that they are in imminent danger of death. In *Owens v HM Advocate* (1946) the accused believed that the deceased was attacking him with a knife and killed him. He was convicted of murder, but on appeal the conviction was quashed on the grounds that the appellant's belief that he was in imminent danger was held on reasonable grounds. Lord Justice General Normand stated (at p.125) that

"self defence is made out when it is established to the satisfaction of the jury that the [accused] believed that he was in imminent danger and that he held that belief on reasonable grounds. Grounds for such belief may exist though they are founded on a genuine mistake of fact."

A mistaken belief in respect of a fatal attack must be both honest and reasonable (*Lieser v HM Advocate* (2008)).

Self–defence and property
There is not a great deal of Scottish authority on whether self-defence can be used in defence of property, however, in *McCluskey* (discussed above), Lord Clyde implicitly excludes killing in the defence of property in his description of when self-defence could be pled. It is unlikely that a person who struggles with a thief who is trying to steal a bag will be charged with assault, but if a housebreaker had used no violence but was severely assaulted with, e.g. a weapon, the situation would differ and self-defence would not be available.

Is self-defence available where the accused has started a fight?
Self-defence may be pled by a person who has started an altercation. The normal rules of self-defence, outlined above, would apply in these circumstances. In *Boyle v HM Advocate* (1993) the court held that the trial judge had misdirected the jury when he said the appellant could not plead self-defence if he willingly joined the fight he was involved in. The court held that the availability of self-defence would depend on the circumstances. This was followed in *Burns v HM Advocate* (1995), which reiterated that the issue is whether the victim's response to the accused's initial violence is of the quality to place the accused in immediate danger of death and that he then responds proportionately when there is no reasonable means of escape.

(5) Automatism
A person who acts in a state of unconsciousness or grossly impaired consciousness may be said to act as an automaton and a defence of automatism may be available. Automatism cases commonly involve somnambulism, diabetes, epileptic seizure and the effect of ingesting certain types of drugs. Section 78(2) of the CPSA 1995 defined automatism as a special defence. The question of automatism is rather complex. The first issue that should be noted is that automatism is distinct from mental disorder. The latter requires mental illness or a mental disorder that results in a total alienation of reason; automatism, on the other hand, is where the accused's mental state is caused by external factors. Automatism was not recognised as a defence prior to 1991 and to operate as a defence very strict conditions must be complied with. The defence has been interpreted to negate the mens rea of the accused rather than the actus reus. This has implications for those strict liability offences where mens rea does not require to be proven.

Requirements of automatism prior to Ross
Until *Ross v HM Advocate* (1991) the law in Scotland, in respect of automatic acts, was governed by *HM Advocate v Cunningham* (1963). In *Cunningham*, the accused was charged with taking a motorvan, causing

death by dangerous driving and being unfit to drive through drink or drugs. He lodged a special defence, which stated (at p.80) that

> "throughout the period during which the crimes libelled are said to have been committed he was not responsible for his actings on account of the incidence of temporary dissociation due to an epileptic fugue or other pathological condition."

Lord Justice General Clyde (at p.83) rejected that this was a competent special defence at all and stated that these factors only had a bearing upon mitigation of sentence and not upon guilt. He said that to be accepted as a special defence this would require an averment of insanity (now called mental disorder) at the time the offence was committed. He stated (at p.84) that:

> "Any mental or pathological condition short of insanity—any question of diminished responsibility owing to any cause, which does not involve insanity—is relevant only to the question of mitigating circumstances and sentence."

In *Cunningham* the Crown argued that *HM Advocate v Ritchie* (1926), where the defence of temporary mental dissociation due to toxic exhaust fumes was accepted as a special defence, could be distinguished due to the exhaust fumes being an external factor. Lord Clyde concluded, however, that *Ritchie* had been wrongly decided.

The effect of the decision in *Cunningham* was that, unless temporary mental dissociation met the legal requirements of the defence of insanity (with the consequences, prior to the 1995 Act, of detention in hospital), it could not mitigate responsibility but only the punishment of the accused. Therefore, those who committed crimes while in a state of involuntary intoxication, concussion, epilepsy or diabetes had no defence available to them. This was even though they clearly lacked the necessary mens rea to commit crimes and their actions were not in any sense voluntary. *Ross v HM Advocate* (1991) has partially overruled *Cunningham* but there remain circumstances, e.g. where the accused's actions are the result of an internal condition, such as epilepsy or diabetes, when *Cunningham* remains the authoritative case.

Ross v HM Advocate

In *Ross* the accused was charged with a number of assaults. His defence was that his drink had been "spiked" with hallucinogenic and tranquillising drugs; that he did not know his drink had been spiked and that it was this which had caused his violent conduct. The defence argued that the effect of the drugs was to deprive the accused of his self-control to such an extent that he was incapable of forming mens rea and that it should be left to the jury to consider whether or not they should acquit him on this ground. The trial judge directed the jury, in accordance with *Cunningham*, that the evidence of the accused's mental state at the time could not result in acquittal. Ross was convicted and appealed on the grounds that the jury had been misdirected to convict the accused, that the judge was wrong in holding that he was bound by *Cunningham* and, if *Cunningham* was held to apply, it should be reconsidered in order that a defence of non-culpable automatism be admissible.

The court noted that senior counsel for the appellant did not seek to challenge the soundness of *Cunningham* on its own facts. Lord Justice General Hope noted (at p.213) that "in principle it would seem that in all cases where a person lacks the evil intention which is essential to the guilt of crime he must be acquitted". Two exceptions to this principle were identified. Senior counsel and the judges recognised that where the mental condition which is said to affect mens rea is a pathological condition which might recur, it must, for reasons of public policy, be the subject of a special defence of insanity. Lord Hope also stated (at p.214) that where the absence of mens rea is self-induced the accused must, for public policy reasons, be assumed to have intended the natural consequences of his act.

However, the court in *Ross* emphasised that there was no challenge to *Cunningham* on its facts, as *Ross* was concerned with a mental condition of a temporary nature, which was the result of an external factor, which was not self-induced, and it did not involve a disorder of the mind that was liable to recur. In *Ross* Lord Hope (at p.218) provided the following requirements before automatism would result in acquittal and stated that these should provide adequate safeguards against abuse. The requirements are:

(a)   it must not be self-induced;
(b)   it must be one which the accused was not bound to foresee; and
(c)   the external factor must have resulted in a total alienation of reason amounting to a complete absence of self-control.

The defence of automatism created in *Ross* was clarified in the case *Sorley v HM Advocate* (1992). *Sorley* established that the evidential burden on the accused who pleads this defence is a heavy one. There must be expert evidence of a total alienation of reason leading to a complete loss of self-control and the evidence must show that the accused did not know the nature of his actions.

Effect of Ross

The effect of the decision in *Ross* was to partially overturn the decision in *Cunningham*. As a result, any internal condition, e.g. epilepsy, diabetes or parasomnia (sleepwalking), which is the cause of an automatic state will only be relevant in determining sentence and not responsibility, unless the accused also happens to be insane when they commit the offence. As noted above, where an automatic state is the result of self-induced intoxication by alcohol or drugs, even where intoxication has induced a state such as sleepwalking, the defence of automatism is not available to an accused

(*Finegan v Heywood* (2000); *Ebsworth v HM Advocate* (1992)). Individuals who offend during an epileptic seizure have generally been regarded as suffering from an internal condition (*HM Advocate v Mitchell* (1951)).

The matter is more complicated where a diabetic person offends as a result of insulin-induced hypoglycaemia. *Ross* suggested that hypoglycaemia is not a proper basis for a defence of automatism but this was not followed in *MacLeod v Mathieson* (1993), where there was doubt over whether the hypoglycaemia was caused by insulin or diabetes and the sheriff was prepared to accept that hypoglycaemia was an external factor. The defence was not successful, however, as it was deemed that the accused should have foreseen the external factor and its effects. In *HM Advocate v Watret* (2000) Lord Nimmo Smith directed the jury that, as far as he was aware, this was the first time the High Court had considered the defence of automatism arising from alleged hypoglycaemia. The accused was indicted on four charges of breach of the peace and one charge of aggravated assault and attempted murder. Three of the breach of the peace charges related to the period when the accused was on bail, pending his trial for aggravated assault and attempted murder charges. In the course of an argument, Watret had attacked his wife with a Stanley knife which resulted in her being permanently scarred. The accused's defence was that he was in a hypoglycaemic state at the time of the attack. The advocate-depute invited the judge to direct the jury that the special defence of automatism was not open for their consideration. The judge repelled this submission and directed the jury on the three requirements of automatism. The jury were asked to decide whether hypoglycaemia is ever capable of amounting to automatism. In particular, they were asked to consider:

(1)   Whether insulin could properly be described as an external factor and, while it may be self-administered, as it is not in general taken for the purposes of causing hypoglycaemia, is it self-induced? (This question was to address whether the taking of the insulin was an external factor that was not self-induced.)

(2)   Was the accused bound to foresee the possibility of insulin as an external factor, causing such a degree of hypoglycaemia as to result in a total alienation of reason, amounting to a total loss of control of his actions? To answer this question the jury were asked to consider his level of knowledge and what advice had been given to the accused about matters such as the interval of time between taking insulin and taking food, the effects of alcohol on blood sugar levels, and so on. (This question was to ascertain whether the effects of the insulin were reasonably foreseeable.)

(3)   In light of the expert evidence, whether a hypoglycaemic attack amounts to a total alienation of reason. (This question is to establish if the effect of the insulin was to cause a total alienation of reason.)

The accused was found guilty of two of the breach of the peace charges and the aggravated assault charge under deletion of "to the danger of life and you did attempt to murder her" with the added rider "whilst in a hypoglycaemic state". The jury clearly did not accept that the accused fulfilled the requirements of the automatism defence or they would have acquitted him. Nevertheless, Lord Nimmo Smith did say that the rider was taken into account in passing a sentence of imprisonment of three years.

(6) Coercion

Coercion arises where one person has forced another to commit a crime. It may operate either as a defence or in mitigation. It is now classified as a special defence by the CPSA 1995 s.78(2).

The rules of the defence are outlined by Hume (I, 51) as:

(a)   there must be an immediate danger of death or great bodily harm;
(b)   an inability to resist the violence;
(c)   a backward and inferior part in the perpetration; and
(d)   a disclosure of the fact, as well as restitution of the spoil, on the first safe and convenient occasion.

In *Thomson v HM Advocate* (1983) the appellant was convicted art and part with another man of assault and armed robbery. Thomson claimed that on the outward journey he didn't know he was driving his co-accused to commit a robbery. When he found out and tried to leave, a gun was produced which went off when he tried to get out of the van, and he was shot on the hand. His defence was that he had been coerced into taking part in the assault and robbery. The question of coercion was left to the jury and Lord Hunter directed them on Hume's requirements for coercion and emphasised that there must be an immediate danger of death or great bodily harm. The jury convicted both accused. Thomson appealed on the ground that the judge had misdirected the jury as to the requirements of the defence of coercion. Refusing the appeal, Lord Justice Clerk Wheatley stated (at pp.77–78) that

> "the four 'qualifications' to which [Hume] refers are tests of the validity of such a defence. The first two are conditions to be satisfied before the defence gets off the ground. It is only if it does get off the ground that the other two tests come into play as a measure of the accused's credibility and reliability on the issue of the defence."

Before coercion will be available as a defence:

(a)   The accused must have acted in the face of an immediate threat of death or great bodily harm (*Trotter v HM Advocate* (2001)). In *Trotter* the court held that the appellant had the opportunity to inform the authorities of his situation but chose not to do so because he was afraid. The court held that although such circumstances cannot amount to a complete defence, they may, if accepted, be taken into account in mitigation of sentence.

(b)   The accused must have been unable to resist the threat against him. In deciding whether or not an individual should have been able to resist a threat against him, subjective characteristics will not be taken into account. Instead, an objective test is applied to determine whether the threats made were such as would have overcome the resolution of an ordinarily constituted person of the same age and sex (*Cochrane v HM Advocate* (2001)). In *Cochrane* the appeal court rejected the argument that the court should have taken into account that the accused had a very low IQ and was unusually susceptible as far as compliance was concerned when considering whether Cochrane could have reasonably been expected to resist a particular threat.

(c)   The defence of coercion may be excluded where the accused has voluntarily exposed himself to the risk of coercion by, for example, joining a criminal or terrorist organisation. The issue has not arisen directly; however, the judge in *Thomson v HM Advocate* (1983) excludes the availability of the defence of coercion in these circumstances.

Coercion and murder
It is unclear whether coercion would ever be a valid defence to murder. In *Thomson* Lord Justice Clerk Wheatley stated (at p.78):

> "[A] defence of coercion is recognised in the law of Scotland. Doubts have been expressed on whether it extends to murder cases, but that does not arise here and we express no opinion on that point. Hume restricts it to 'atrocious crimes', and whether a particular crime falls into that category will depend not only on the nature of the crime but on its attendant circumstances."

In *Collins v HM Advocate* (1991) Lord Allanbridge directed the jury (at p.902) that "as a matter of law coercion is not a defence in Scotland to the crime of murder".

OTHER DEFENCES

In addition to the "special defences" outlined above, there are other defences which do not require notice to be given to the court. The defences in this group serve to mitigate responsibility of the accused but do not result in acquittal.

Diminished responsibility
Diminished responsibility, unlike insanity, does not result in the acquittal of the accused but only mitigates the accused's responsibility. The doctrine of diminished responsibility, rather than the term, first appeared in *HM Advocate v Dingwall* (1867). The modern doctrine of diminished

responsibility was regarded as being found in *HM Advocate v Savage* (1923) and required aberration or weakness of mind, some form of mental unsoundness, a mind bordering on though not amounting to insanity, a mind so affected that responsibility is diminished from full to partial responsibility and there must be some form of mental disease. Until *Galbraith v HM Advocate* (2001) the direction to the jury in *Savage* was deemed to be authoritative. In *Galbraith* the court held that, while the plea of diminished responsibility will only be available where the accused's abnormality of mind had substantial effects in relation to his act, there was no requirement that his state of mind should have bordered on insanity. In terms of an appropriate direction to a jury on the question of diminished responsibility, it is stated that this should no longer simply recite the *Savage* formula, quoted above, but should be tailored as far as possible to the facts of the particular case (at p.552):

> "[I]n essence, the jury should be told that they must be satisfied that, by reason of the abnormality of mind in question, the ability of the accused, as compared with a normal person, to determine or control his actings was substantially impaired."

Galbraith's murder conviction was quashed and a re-trial was ordered. At the re-trial she pled guilty to a reduced charge of culpable homicide on the basis that she suffered from diminished responsibility when she killed her husband (she had given evidence at her trial that he had been abusive to her). The relaxing of the requirements of diminished responsibility in *Galbraith* led to it being used by the majority of women subsequently charged with the murder of an abusive partner.

This common law partial defence was codified by the CJLSA 2010 and the relevant common law rules shall cease to have effect. The provision is contained within s.51B of the CPSA 1995. This provision largely restates the requirements of the defence as stated in *Galbraith* except that a psychopathic personality is no longer ruled out as qualifying as an abnormality of mind. Diminished responsibility therefore has two requirements:

(1) An abnormality of mind. This includes mental disorder. It does not include intoxication (s.51B(3)) but psychopathic personality is not ruled out.
(2) The accused has a resultant substantial impairment of his ability to determine or control his actions. This is a matter of fact for the jury to determine.

The defence is only available in respect of a charge of murder (s.51B(1) of the CPSA 1995) and, where it is successfully pled, results in a conviction of culpable homicide (*HM Advocate v Cunningham* (1963)). When diminished responsibility is pled, the onus of proof is on the defence for the purpose of proving diminished responsibility (s.51(3), (4); *Lilburn v HM*

Advocate (2011)). Diminished responsibility requires to be proven on the balance of probabilities.

Provocation

> "The defence of provocation is of this sort: Being agitated and excited, and alarmed by violence, I lost control over myself, and took life when my presence of mind had left me, and without thought of what I was doing." (Macdonald, *A Practical Treatise on the Criminal Law of Scotland* (5th edn, 1948) p.94.)

The defence of provocation does not result in acquittal but operates as an excuse and will reduce a charge of murder to culpable homicide. In *Drury v HM Advocate* (2001) Lord Justice General Rodger stated (at p.593) that

> "the person who kills under provocation is to be convicted of culpable homicide rather than murder because, even if he intentionally kills his victim, he does not have that wicked intention which is required for murder."

Rules of provocation

(1)   Provocation must be by violence or infidelity.
(2)   Provocation must result in a complete loss of self-control.
(3)   Retaliation must be immediate.
(4)   Retaliation must be proportionate or, in the case of infidelity, that of the reasonable person.

Provocation must be by violence or infidelity. The provocation must be by "real" injury, i.e. violence, and therefore verbal provocation is not enough. The general rule is that verbal provocation is not enough to reduce a charge of murder to culpable homicide (*Cosgrove v HM Advocate* (1991)). Despite this, the courts have sometimes allowed juries to consider verbal provocation. In *Berry v HM Advocate* (1976) the accused was charged with the murder of a woman. He gave evidence that the deceased had taunted him when he had tried unsuccessfully to have intercourse with her and that he had retaliated by striking her on the head with a brick. The trial judge allowed the question of provocation to be decided by the jury and directed them to consider whether these taunts were sufficient provocation for what the accused had done. The accused was convicted and appealed. Rejecting the appeal, the court expressed "grave doubts" regarding this issue having been left to the jury.

The generally accepted position is that verbal provocation is recognised in relation to assault but only where the provocation is immediate inflammatory abuse, which leads to a loss of self-control (*Thomson v HM Advocate* (1985)) but note the comments of the Court of Appeal in

Anderson v HM Advocate (2010) where when considering an appeal against a conviction for murder, the court stated

> "in a case such as the present when it is claimed that the accused was subject to verbal abuse, but was not physically assaulted, provocation can only arise (a) where the accused has been subjected to verbal insult or abuse; (b) where he has lost his temper and self-control immediately; (c) where he retaliated instantly and in hot blood; and (d) where the ordinary person would have acted as the accused did".

Prior to *Anderson v HM Advocate* (2010), and probably still, there is only one recognised exception to the rule that only provocation by physical violence is relevant to a charge of murder. This exception is where the source of the provocation is infidelity and this has been described as "the adultery exception". Hume referred to provocation applying where the accused discovered his wife committing adultery with a man. Later cases also recognised an admission of adultery (*HM Advocate v Hill* (1941)), where the parties were not married but it was deemed that sexual fidelity was owed (*McDermott v HM Advocate* (1974)) and where the couple were of the same sex (*HM Advocate v McKean* (1997)). Any confession of adultery must be "clear and unequivocal" (*HM Advocate v McKean* (1997)) and any such confession must be accepted by the accused (*McCormack v HM Advocate* (1993)).

The law relating to provocation by infidelity has been further clarified in the leading case of *Drury v HM Advocate* (2001). In *Drury* the accused and the deceased had lived together and, although they were living apart at the time of the killing, the defence argued that there was still a relationship between the parties and the accused was entitled to expect sexual fidelity on the part of the deceased. The Crown contested that there was a continuing relationship between the parties. The accused suspected that the deceased had been unfaithful when he saw another man leaving her home. When he confronted her and asked what was going on, she replied, "What do you think?" The accused then attacked the deceased, hitting her on the head with a claw hammer and killed her. He was convicted of murder and appealed on the basis that the trial judge had misdirected the jury that there must be a "reasonable relationship" between the provocation offered and the violence used by the accused. Lord Justice General Rodger stated (at p.597) that the trial judge was wrong to give that direction since "the sexual activity and the appellant's attack on the deceased are actually incommensurable". He accepted the suggestion by the appellant's counsel that the test of proportionality should be rejected and instead the accused's act in killing the deceased would fall to be treated as culpable homicide only if the ordinary man (or woman, as the case may be) would have been liable to act in the same way, in the same circumstances. The appeal was allowed and authority for a new prosecution was granted. At the subsequent trial *HM Advocate v Drury* (Unreported August 2001 Edinburgh High Court) the accused was again charged with murder and pled provocation and diminished responsibility (relying on the decision in *Galbraith v HM Advocate* (2001), referred to above). The jury returned a verdict of guilty of murder.

Provocation must result in a complete loss of self-control. Evidence of a loss of self-control is essential in any plea of provocation (*Low v HM Advocate* (1994)). In addition to evidence, however, it also must be established that such a loss of self-control was reasonable. This has traditionally been tested objectively by reference to the reasonable person test.

This objective test, based on the ordinary person, does not take into account the characteristics of the accused. In other jurisdictions the accused's characteristics are considered in respect of both the effect of and the reaction to provocation, e.g. *R. v Camplin* (1978). In those cases where the accused's characteristics are taken into account a subjective test is employed.

Retaliation must be immediate. As any retaliation must be immediate, any time lapse between the provocation and retaliation may suggest that the accused has regained control and is merely taking revenge. Cumulative provocation is not recognised and, therefore, there must be a final provoking act before events that have occurred in the past are deemed relevant. This is particularly problematic where there has been a relationship between the accused and the deceased involving abuse and violence. In this situation, the perpetrator of fatal violence may anticipate, through past experience, that the deceased will become violent and act almost pre-emptively.

The difficulty in such a scenario is that the past violence is not recognised as being a reasonable basis to anticipate future events, nor is it deemed to amount to cumulative provocation in the absence of a final act of violence. Such a scenario is found in cases where women kill abusive men. In *HM Advocate v June Greig* (1979) there was a history of abuse by the deceased towards his wife. On the night he was killed, the husband had been verbally, although not physically, abusive and the accused's evidence was that she anticipated he would become violent. The judge in this case withdrew self-defence from the jury and directed the jury that there were no grounds for provocation. The jury, clearly ignoring his direction, returned a verdict of culpable homicide.

Retaliation must be proportionate. The retaliation to physical or verbal provocation must be proportionate (*Gillon v HM Advocate* (2007)). In determining the requirements of proportionate retaliation, the courts, in the past, adopted a similar approach to that used in respect of self-defence. For both self-defence and provocation, therefore, if an accused had acted with "cruel excess" neither provocation nor self-defence was available to them. In *Lennon v HM Advocate* (1991) (at p.614F) Lord Justice General Hope refers to "cruel excess, or a gross disproportion between the provocation offered and the retaliation" as excluding provocation. Subsequent case law suggests that the preferred test for provocation is "gross disproportion" (*Robertson v HM Advocate* (1994)). This matter is more complex where the provocation is the discovery of adultery, which is considered below. In respect of provocation by infidelity, the Appeal Court has stated that the proportionality test should not be used and, instead, the question is whether the accused reacted as an ordinary person might have done (*Drury v HM Advocate* (2001)). In *Drury* Lord Justice General Rodger stated (at p.599):

> "[I]f there is evidence of a relationship entitling the accused to expect sexual fidelity on the part of the deceased, the jury should be directed to consider two matters. First, they should consider whether, at the time when he killed the deceased, the accused had in fact lost his self-control as a result of the preceding provocation. If they conclude that he had not lost his self-control, then the plea of provocation must fail and the jury will have to consider, on the basis of all the rest of the evidence, whether the appropriate verdict is one of murder or culpable homicide. If, on the other hand, the jury come to the conclusion that he had indeed lost his self-control due to the provocation, then they should ask themselves whether an ordinary man, having been thus provoked, would have been liable to react as he did."

Intoxication

The general rule is that voluntary intoxication is not a defence to a criminal act (*Brennan v HM Advocate* (1977); *Donaldson v Normand* (1997)), nor must it be taken into account in sentencing by way of mitigation (CJLSA 2010 s.23A(2)).

In *Ross v HM Advocate* (1991) the court stated:

> "[W]here the condition which has resulted in an absence of mens rea is self-induced ... the accused must be assumed to have intended the natural consequences of his act."

The situation of involuntary intoxication is clearly different. In *HM Advocate v Raiker* (1989) Lord McCluskey said an accused would lack the criminal state of mind that is a necessary ingredient of any crime where he had acted wholly and completely under the influence of some drug which was administered by force or without his consent.

Necessity

The defence of necessity is used where the accused behaves in a manner which is not legal to avoid another danger. This defence is often used, therefore, where the accused has been coerced by circumstances into breaking the law. The High Court has been willing to recognise this defence, despite Hume's disapproval (I, 54–55), but there are strict requirements to avoid the defence being used in frivolous circumstances.

Recent cases have tended to concentrate on road traffic offences. In

Tudhope v Grubb (1983) the accused paid another man £75 in advance to repair his car. Three months later the repairs had not been carried out and the accused, after six pints of beer, went to visit the man. An argument started and the man and two of his friends assaulted the accused. The accused escaped from the men and got into his car which was then attacked by the men, kicking it and trying to smash the windows. He then tried to drive off in his car but the battery was flat so it would not start. The police arrived and the accused was charged with attempting to drive with an excess of alcohol in his blood. The sheriff held that the accused had attempted to drive in an effort to save himself further injury and that he had made a full disclosure of the facts to the police at the first available opportunity. Finding the defence of necessity established the accused was acquitted.

Subsequent cases illustrate the four conditions of the defence:

(a) there must be immediate danger of death or great bodily harm (*Moss v Howdle* (1997));

(b) there must be no reasonable alternative course of action (*Moss v Howdle* (1997); *D v Donnelly* (2009));

(c) the accused's conduct must have a reasonable prospect of removing or avoiding the danger (*Lord Advocate's Reference (No.1 of 2000)* (2001));

(d) the threat must have dominated the mind of the accused at the time (*Dawson v Dickson* (1999)).

The first two of these conditions come from the case of *Moss v Howdle* (1997). In *Moss* the accused was convicted of speeding on a motorway. He claimed that he thought his passenger was seriously ill and drove to the nearest service station where the passenger told him he was only suffering from an attack of cramp. The sheriff accepted that, in the circumstances, it was reasonable to suspect that the passenger was seriously ill but said that the accused should have found out what was wrong with the passenger, by stopping at the side of the road, before he committed the offence. As another course of action was available, the defence of necessity was not available. On appeal, the court held that the defence of necessity would be available in respect of medical emergencies as well as to avoid violent attacks so long as there was an immediate danger of death or great bodily harm (this is a requirement of both coercion and self-defence). The court also stated that the defence was available to protect a third party, but was not available to the accused in this particular case because an alternative course of action was available to him which did not involve committing an offence. The appeal was refused.

The third condition comes from the *Lord Advocate's Reference (No.1 of 2000)* (2001). The accused had damaged a ship that was involved in supplying submarines that carried nuclear weapons. They were charged with malicious mischief and pled necessity on the basis that their damage of the ship was to prevent a crime being committed, namely a breach of international law by the UK government. The sheriff directed the jury to acquit the accused on the basis of necessity. The Crown brought a Lord Advocate's reference. The court held that the requirements of the defence of necessity were immediacy and response to danger and that the action taken had a reasonable prospect of preventing the supposed danger.

The fourth condition comes from *Dawson v Dickson* (1999). The Appeal Court confirmed that necessity is only available as a defence when there is a dilemma faced by an individual between saving life or avoiding serious bodily harm on the one hand, and breaking the law on the other. The defence is not available to those who act without first considering this dilemma.

Superior orders
A soldier or policeman may have a defence of superior orders, provided he acted within the rules of service and in pursuit of a legal aim (*HM Advocate v Sheppard* (1941)).

Entrapment
Until *Jones and Doyle v HM Advocate* (Appeal Court, High Court of Justiciary, October 30, 2009), the issue of entrapment was deemed to be confined to admissibility of the evidence obtained. In *Jones and Doyle* the court stated that to deal with entrapment as an issue affecting the admissibility of evidence was unsatisfactory. The court held that to prosecute a case on the basis of entrapment is oppressive and unfair to the accused. This is properly a matter to be considered as a plea in bar of trial, but it does not follow that all questions of fairness to an accused will require a plea in bar of trial—less fundamental attacks on the fairness of the circumstances of a particular piece of potential evidence are properly made by raising an issue about the admissibility of that evidence.

READING

T. Jones and M. Christie, *Criminal Law*, 5th edn (Edinburgh: W. Green & Son, 2012), Chs 8 and 9.

C. Gane, C. Stoddart and J. Chalmers, *A Casebook on Scottish Criminal Law*, 4th edn (Edinburgh: W. Green & Son, 2009), Ch.7.

G.H. Gordon, *Criminal Law*, edited by M. Christie, 3rd edn (Edinburgh: W. Green & Son, 2000), Vol. I, Chs 10–13.

APPENDIX: SAMPLE EXAMINATION
QUESTION AND ANSWER

Sarah visits her wealthy grandmother's home. She opens the safe and takes a Rolex watch. She then takes the watch to an insurance company and insures it for £20,000. This insurance policy protects against accidental damage, loss and theft. Before returning the watch to her grandmother's home she asks her friend Ann to take some photographs of her wearing the watch. A month later she reports to the insurance company that she has lost the watch. She follows their instruction of contacting the police and is sent the appropriate claims form. She completes the form and sends it to the insurance company.

Sample Answer
Sarah taking her grandmother's watch, presumably without consent, is theft. If she had the consent of her grandmother no theft would be committed. The current definition of theft can be stated as: *Theft is constituted by the appropriation, without the owner's consent, of any item of corporeal, moveable property, which is in the ownership of another person, with the intention to deprive the owner of that property permanently, temporarily or indefinitely.* The actus reus of theft is appropriation which includes theft achieved by taking and the mens rea is intention to deprive the owner of his property, although it doesn't need to be a permanent deprivation. There is no need for 'profit', it is the owner's loss rather than the other's gain which is important (*Black v Carmichael*; *Carmichael v Black*[1]). The mens rea of intention to deprive the owner of their property can be inferred from the facts of the case. Until relatively recently, the mens rea of theft was understood to be an intention to permanently deprive an owner of their property. Any temporary deprivation was regarded as the lesser crime of clandestinely taking and using the property of another, e.g. *Strathern v Seaforth*.[2] Recent case law shows more flexibility but inconsistency in respect of the mens rea of theft.

The earliest challenge to the accepted rule that permanent deprivation is necessary for the crime of theft is found in *Kivlin v Milne*.[3] Courts have since recognised an intention to deprive temporarily. In *Black v Carmichael*; *Carmichael v Black*[4] the court held that an intention to deprive the owner of their property temporarily will suffice for the crime of theft. Unlike earlier decisions, they do not make reference to temporary deprivation amounting to permanent deprivation (*Kivlin*[5]) nor any requirement for a nefarious purpose to be proven (*Milne v Tudhope*[6]). The opinions delivered in *Black* stress that it is the owner's loss and not the other's gain which is important in relation to the crime of theft. In *Kane v Friel*,[7] the advocate-depute had accepted that the Crown required to prove that the accused must have intended to appropriate the items dishonestly. The current facts allow us to infer that Sarah intended to temporarily deprive her grandmother of the watch. We can also infer from her subsequent actions, covertly taking and returning the watch, insuring it etc., that she had a dishonest intention to deprive her grandmother of her property.

The next issue to consider is whether the taking of the watch involved Sarah overcoming the security of the safe. The facts given suggest that Sarah could access the safe either with the combination or a key. In the absence of evidence of her having to overcome the security of the safe, the charge should only be of theft and not theft by opening a lockfast place.

Sarah then insures the watch and subsequently reports its loss to the insurance company. The crime of fraud has been defined by Macdonald as the "bringing about of any practical result by false pretences",[8] but this is only a statement of the actus reus.

The actus reus of fraud requires a false pretence,[9] a practical result[10] and a causal link between the false pretence and the practical result. The mens rea requires that the accused acted intentionally with the knowledge that the pretence was false. The completed crime requires that the third party is deceived and acts in a way they would not otherwise have done without the false pretence (*Cummings v HM Advocate* and *McPhee v HM Advocate*[11]).

Fraud is a result crime. It does not appear that the insurance company have yet paid any money to Sarah in respect of her claim. The appropriate charge should therefore be attempted fraud. No exact point in the perpetration of a crime has been identified in case law as amounting to the actus reus of an attempted crime and three theories have been relied upon, namely, the irrevocability theory (*HM Advocate v Tannahill and Neilson*[12]), the last act theory (*Samuel Tumbelson*[13]) and perpetration theory (*HM Advocate v Cameron*[14]). Perpetration theory has been preferred in more recent cases. In *HM Advocate v Cameron*, Lord Justice General Dunedin said, at p.485, that the essential question was where preparation ends and perpetration begins " ...but if that scheme is so carried out as that a false insurance is taken, and that a false robbery is gone through, very little more will do". In Sarah's case the insurance claim has been made but not yet settled, so she should be charged with attempted fraud.

The question states that Ann took photographs of Sarah wearing the watch. Art and part responsibility arises where two or more individuals participate in the commission of a crime either as a result of a prior common plan (*HM Advocate v Fraser and Rollins*[15]) or spontaneously (*Gallacher v HM Advocate*[16]). Art and part guilt can arise from different types of participation in a criminal purpose but as a minimum the parties must know that the crime is being committed. The facts of the question do not suggest that Ann had such knowledge. It is possible to establish art and part responsibility on the basis of material assistance, but it must be shown that the parties have participated in a common plan to commit a crime. However, any assistance must have been provided prior to the commission of the crime. Although the provider of assistance need not be aware of every aspect of the crime planned or have participated in the commission of the crime, it is clear that they must be aware that they are assisting a criminal purpose. There must also be some connection between the actual perpetrator of the harm and the assistance provider. It is not clear from the facts that when Ann took the photographs of Sarah's watch she knew that she was assisting in a common plan or purpose to commit a crime. The photographs were taken prior to the insurance claim being made and therefore the assistance was provided prior to the commission of the crime. Whether Ann should be charged art and part with Sarah with the crime of attempted fraud is dependent on whether she knew she was assisting Sarah in committing the crime.

---

[1]   1992 S.L.T. 897.
[2]   1926 J.C. 100.
[3]   1979 S.L.T. (Notes) 2.
[4]   1992 S.L.T. 897.
[5]   1979 S.L.T. (Notes) 2.
[6]   1981 J.C. 53.
[7]   1997 J.C. 69.
[8]   J.H.A. Macdonald, *A Practical Treatise on the Criminal Law of Scotland*, edited by J. Walker and D.J. Stevenson, 5th edn (Edinburgh: W. Green, 1948), p.52.
[9]   James Paton (1858) 3 Irv 208.
[10] The recipient of any false pretence must be deceived by it, *William Fraser* (1847) Ark. 280.
[11] *Cummings v HM Advocate* [2009] HCJAC 55 and *McPhee v HM Advocate*, 2009 J.C. 308.
[12] 1943 J.C. 150.
[13] (1863) 4 Irv. 426.
[14] (1911) 6 Adam 456.
[15] 1920 J.C. 60.
[16] 1951 J.C. 38.

Author's Note

I remain indebted to those who assisted in the production of the previous editions of this text. The views and any errors expressed in this text are the sole responsibility of the author. Additional sample questions and answers are available in the previous editions of this text. This edition is dedicated to Lala, Steff, Belle and Luca.

INDEX